A PLACE CALLED HOME

A Place Called Home

THE SOCIAL DIMENSIONS OF HOMEOWNERSHIP

Kim R. Manturuk

Mark R. Lindblad

and Roberto G. Quercia

OXFORD
UNIVERSITY PRESS

Oxford University Press is a department of the University of Oxford. It furthers
the University's objective of excellence in research, scholarship, and education
by publishing worldwide. Oxford is a registered trade mark of Oxford University
Press in the UK and certain other countries.

Published in the United States of America by Oxford University Press
198 Madison Avenue, New York, NY 10016, United States of America.

Library of Congress Cataloging-in-Publication Data
Names: Manturuk, Kim R., author. | Lindblad, Mark R., author. |
Quercia, Roberto G., 1953– author.
Title: A place called home: the social dimensions of homeownership /
Kim R. Manturuk, Mark R. Lindblad, Roberto G. Quercia.
Description: New York, NY : Oxford University Press, [2017] |
Includes bibliographical references and index.
Identifiers: LCCN 2016054329 (print) | LCCN 2017014065 (ebook) |
ISBN 9780190653255 (updf) | ISBN 9780190653248 (alk. paper)
Subjects: LCSH: Home ownership—Social aspects—United States. | Homeowners—United States.
Classification: LCC HD7287.82.U6 (ebook) | LCC HD7287.82.U6 M36 2017 (print) |
DDC 333.33/80973—dc23
LC record available at https://lccn.loc.gov/2016054329

9 8 7 6 5 4 3 2 1

Printed by Sheridan Books, Inc., United States of America

To America's children, with the hope that their imaginations will allow them to find answers to the problems we adults seem unable to solve.

Contents

Acknowledgments

THE CENTER FOR Community Capital at the University of North Carolina at Chapel Hill conducts research that helps policymakers, advocates, and the private sector find sustainable ways to broaden economic opportunity. Since 1999, the Center has undertaken research on loans made to low- and moderate-income borrowers through a groundbreaking partnership between Self-Help (a leading community development financial institution based in Durham, North Carolina), the Ford Foundation, and Fannie Mae. This partnership provides an unparalleled opportunity for evaluating the benefits and costs of affordable home lending. This fight for the economic rights of lower-income people inspires our work and is an asset to the field.

Without the help, support, and guidance of many others, this project would not have been possible. These contributions only made the book better; any remaining shortcomings and errors are entirely our own. In particular, we'd like to thank the following people.

First and foremost, we acknowledge and thank Frank DeGiovanni and George McCarthy, both formerly of the Ford Foundation, and Michael A. Stegman, Founding Director of the Center. Their deep, thoughtful, and generous support over many years has made this work possible. Further, they have contributed substantively to our analysis by pushing us to question our assumptions, improve our data-collection practices, and strengthen our analysis. Neither the Center nor this book would exist today without their groundbreaking vision and tireless work.

In particular, we recognize Center researchers Sarah Riley and Allison Freeman, who have produced rigorous studies on the economic and social impacts of home-ownership. Their work has also contributed directly to the data and analysis in this book. We also value the scholarship, help, and colleagueship of Janneke Ratcliffe, Lucy Gorham, Jess Dorrance, and Mark McDaniel.

We further recognize the important contribution of many here at UNC. Catherine Zimmer of the Odum Institute provided ongoing statistical guidance. Dozens of graduate students worked for the Center and helped in various ways; we thank especially Huifang Zhao and Zhen Qi. Additionally, we thank Amy Bullington for assisting with the prospectus and Cara Isher-Witt for her close editing during the final stages of this project.

Allison Freeman provided invaluable assistance as the developmental editor of this project and her hard work culminated in a preliminary draft of this book. We are also deeply grateful to Julia Barnard, a Research Associate at the Center, who helped us present this book to potential editors and publishing houses and who ushered it through the contract, revision, and final submission processes.

We are very thankful for the Oxford University Press and their careful steward-ship of this project. In particular, we are grateful for the work and counsel of Dana Bliss, Andrew Dominello, and the anonymous reviewers whose careful comments helped us strengthen the book.

Lastly, research is not possible without data. We thank Martin Eakes, Deborah Momsen-Hudson, Julie Russell, Anne Davis, Tracy Cox, Eric Stein, David Shumannfang, and others at Self-Help for hosting research summits, sharing mortgage data, and contributing to our collaborative inquiry on the issues of housing and homeownership; without their doing so, we would not have a real-world context within which to answer our research questions.

Most of the research in this book uses household survey data, and for that information we are indebted to the former UNC's Survey Research Unit and RTI International. In particular, we thank William Kalsbeek, Robert Agans, Brian Burke, Kathleen Considine, Laura Flicker, Barbara Bibb, and Lauren Warren at RTI International for their efforts in collecting survey data. We also thank the phone and field interviewers who talked with survey participants. Most importantly, we thank the survey respondents who have shared their personal views and experiences.

Foreword

IN THE LATE 1990s, the Ford Foundation made the bold decision to reorient its efforts to combat poverty and injustice by shifting from strategies that supplemented the incomes of poor and low-income people and communities to those that focused on building their assets. This strategy shift was centered on the hypothesis that asset-based interventions had a better chance of making durable improvements in the lives and prospects of low-income people and their families than income subsidies that only would carry them from year to year. The Foundation believed that assisting poor people and communities to acquire, control, and maintain four types of assets—financial, human capital, social, and natural resources—was crucial to reducing poverty because assets have the potential to assist families to generate income, provide a cushion against risk and hard times, improve individual capabilities to succeed, create individual stakes in collective vision and action, and provide a head start for the next generation. Taken as a bundle, these assets would help households achieve an important measure of stability and serve as a platform for upward mobility, enabling households to invest in their future.

Nowhere was the Foundation's strategy shift more radical than in its housing program. After more than two decades of field-building investments in community development focused on the production of affordable rental housing, which included the creation of the first Community Development Corporations (CDCs), and support for research and community organizing to promote important policy tools like the Community Reinvestment Act (CRA) and Low-Income Housing Tax Credits, the Foundation refocused its housing work on promoting homeownership for low-income families as a way to build wealth. This was predicated, in large part, on the fact that housing wealth represented an outsized share of household assets, particularly for low-income homeowners.

Homeownership has long been a centerpiece of housing policy in the United States. It is institutionalized in the preferential tax treatment of homeowners and in federal government interventions in the mortgage finance system dating back to the 1930s. This preference drove the growth of national homeownership rates from less than 44% in 1940 to nearly 70% in 2005, three years prior to the onset of the Great Recession in 2008. However, this impressive growth of homeownership masked substantial disparities in homeownership rates among income and racial groups. For example, in 1993, the homeownership rate for high-income households—those with incomes greater than 120% of area median income—was 84.4%, compared to 44.4% for households with incomes below 50% of the area median income and 57.8% for households with incomes between 50% and 80% of area median income. The disparity in homeownership among racial groups was similarly striking. In 1997, more than 72% of white households owned their own homes, compared to 45.4% for African-Americans and 43.3% for Hispanics (Herbert, Haurin, Rosenthal, & Duda 2005).

These substantial differences in homeownership rates were reflected in dramatic wealth gaps that existed then and persist today. In 1992, lower-income families had less than 5% of the net worth of upper-income families (Fry & Kochar 2014). Similarly, minority households—both African-Americans and Hispanics—had approximately 10% of the net worth of white families in 1993 (Kochar, Fry, & Taylor 2011).

By increasing homeownership opportunities for low-income and minority families, the Foundation believed it would help them to build financial assets both through paying down their mortgages and, hopefully, through increases in the value of their homes. This growing home equity also could serve as a platform for family upward mobility, as households could use home equity to finance small businesses or the education of their children. But we were also excited about the prospect of contributing to the development of the human and social assets that many people believed accompanied the financial benefits of homeownership. These assets—self-efficacy, more cohesive social networks, physical health, mental health, and greater engagement in the community—had not been well-documented in research on homeownership. If we could show that homeowners exhibited positive physical and mental health outcomes, greater levels of participation in the civic life of their communities, expanded social networks, a sense of community, and a willingness to solve problems, then promoting homeownership could be justified further for its contribution to the quality of life and the resilience of families and communities.

As a national foundation, we aspired to achieve impact at scale by changing the way that systems—public policies and markets—operated, since these usually caused and perpetuated the problems that we sought to address. In the case of housing, contradictory elements of the CRA and federal efforts to expand access to housing finance through mortgage securitization impeded access to homeownership for low-income households. The CRA required regulated financial institutions to extend mortgage credit to underserved households and neighborhoods in the financial institutions' designated service areas. To meet their affirmative obligation to extend credit to new populations and areas, lenders began to experiment with new mortgage products and lending channels during the 1990s. The banks partnered with CDCs to cultivate new homebuyers by supporting homeownership education and counseling programs and offered mortgages at very favorable terms. The mortgages were priced at or below the interest rates for prime borrowers and had relaxed underwriting requirements. Typically, lenders required much smaller down payments, often as low as 3%, and they expanded acceptable debt-to-income ratios so that low-income and minority borrowers could qualify for the loans. These lenders assumed that the screening, preparation, and on-going support of the borrowers by their partner CDCs would help to overcome some of the mortgage risk. But, these mortgages did not conform to the more stringent underwriting standards required by Fannie Mae and its sister organization, Freddie Mac, for sale into the secondary market. Thus, banks that made the loans were required to hold them on their own balance sheets, which severely limited the scale of these private market efforts to provide homeownership opportunities to low-income and minority homebuyers. And we were searching for an opportunity to address these systemic barriers to homeownership opportunities for low-income and minority families.

The Self-Help Ventures Fund, the lending arm of a then-small and particularly entrepreneurial North Carolina nonprofit community development financial institution, presented us with an innovative solution to this problem. It wanted to expand a successful pilot program that it had created in North Carolina to purchase $20 million worth of affordable home loans from a local bank under the condition that the bank use the proceeds to extend an equivalent volume of affordable mortgages to other low-income and minority families. The repayment record for the pilot mortgages was so successful that Self-Help had convinced Fannie Mae to use this pilot as a model to expand homeownership nationally to credit-worthy low-income and minority working families.

There was just one catch. To conform to secondary market purchase conditions, Fannie Mae required Self-Help to provide limited recourse on the loans, e.g., to take the first loss if the borrowers defaulted on their loans. Self-Help needed $50 million to increase its net worth to meet this condition in order to create a national secondary market for home mortgages made by CRA lenders. Self-Help turned to us for the $50 million to launch the Community Advantage Program (CAP), then the largest homeownership demonstration in the U.S. and, at the time, the largest grant ever made by the Ford Foundation. This partnership involving Self-Help, Fannie Mae, and the Ford Foundation thus provided us with an amazing opportunity to expand homeownership opportunities for low-income and minority families at a national scale and to identify whether homeownership produced the expected financial and non-financial benefits.

CAP was relatively simple in concept—Self-Help would purchase the non-conforming single-family mortgages that banks made to low-income and minority borrowers and Self-Help would then sell them to Fannie Mae, guaranteeing their performance—although it was a little more complicated in execution. Based on financial projections, the partnership would guarantee the sale of $2 billion of non-conforming mortgages to Fannie Mae, which would result in another $2 billion in additional mortgages made by the partner banks. Fannie Mae and Self-Help projected that this would expand homeownership opportunities to at least 40,000 low-income and minority families. While this was a very important objective for the program, we also had a more far-reaching goal. If CAP's national roll-out proved to be as successful as its North Carolina predecessor, we hoped that Fannie Mae would adopt more relaxed underwriting standards permanently to make it easier for banks to make loans for low-income and minority households to purchase homes.

We put in place a rigorous research project to evaluate the impact of CAP, because so little evidence was available to document the performance of CRA mortgages for low-income and minority households or the financial and social impacts of homeownership on these families. As soon as CAP became operational, we funded the Center for Community Capital at the University of North Carolina (UNC) to track the experience of the households who received CAP loans. We wanted to understand, in as comprehensive and detailed a way as possible, whether and how low-income and minority families benefited from home-ownership. We hoped that these results would alleviate concerns that owning a home exposed low-income people to excessive stress and risk. Equally important, we hoped to demonstrate that the actual credit risk associated with providing mortgages on these terms was much lower than the risks perceived by the lending industry.

Since 1999, the University of North Carolina research team closely monitored the performance of each of the 46,000 affordable home loans involved in the demonstration. Center researchers also interviewed a representative sample of more than 1,800 homeowners each year for 12 years to learn what the opportunity to buy a home with a CAP mortgage had meant for their household. A comparison sample of more than 800 low-income renters also was interviewed each year for 11 years to determine whether the benefits of homeownership were attributable to self-selection rather than tenure choice. Quite unexpectedly, the research has turned out to be a very robust test of the impacts of homeownership and the resilience of homeowners, as the data collection period brackets the incredible run-up of housing prices in many markets due to the creation of, and then the bursting of, the "housing bubble" and the onset of the financial crisis in 2008, with the ensuing collapse of housing prices in many of the same markets. We followed the owners and renters through the end of the Great Recession to observe whether, and how, they were affected by this dramatic downturn in the market.

Given the tumultuous times of the study period, punctuated by a foreclosure crisis that rivaled that of the Great Depression, the results are nothing short of stunning. As first reported in the 2011 book by the UNC research team, *Regaining the Dream: How to Renew the Promise of Homeownership for America's Working Families*, estimates of the economic benefits of homeownership for the homeowners were impressive. As of the third quarter of 2016, borrowers with incomes that averaged $31,000 at loan origination (or 60% of the local area median income) enjoyed a median increase in housing equity of nearly $34,000. Given their small down payments, their annualized return on equity was an incredible 21%. And these were households that otherwise would not have qualified for a mortgage, or would have been provided low-quality loans from subprime lenders. More than half of the borrowers (57%) had credit scores below 680, meaning that they would not have qualified for prime credit. Importantly, owning a home was a much better financial decision than renting. The median user cost of owning a CAP property was $51,700 for the period 2003 to 2011, much less than the estimated median cumulative cost of $78,700 for renting a comparable property (Riley, Ru, & Feng 2013).

The non-financial assets generated by homeownership, as documented in this volume, reinforce for us the importance of successful homeownership in the lives of CAP borrowers. Homeownership is shown to provide households with better access to social capital through expanded social networks. Homeowners also exhibit higher levels of collective efficacy, or the willingness and ability to solve problems. And there was a surprising result in the evaluation regarding the voting behavior and civic participation of homeowners. Not only were homeowners found to be more frequent voters, but homeowners who lived in disadvantaged neighborhoods were found to be more likely to vote in local elections than both homeowners in more advantaged areas and renters in similar neighborhoods. In the words of the researchers, "homeownership may act as a catalyst for political participation in disadvantaged neighborhoods." These are heartwarming results for those of us working toward a primary goal of helping those afflicted by social and economic challenges to participate in solving their own problems.

Other evidence about the non-financial benefits of homeownership provide a more troubling take on the impact of the foreclosure crisis. For example, the research shows that CAP homeowners enjoy better physical and mental health outcomes than the comparison group of renters. The research also shows that the lower levels of mental health impairment for owners is an outgrowth of the sense of control they gained over their lives through owning their homes. But, the research also reveals the evanescence of these health benefits. When facing financial crises, homeowners exhibited more dramatic declines in physical health than renters.

These findings underline the critical importance of "homeownership done right," e.g. homeownership that is financed by responsible lending products and buttressed by a thoughtful and effective lending process with good pre-purchase preparation of borrowers and effective post-purchase assistance to avoid catastrophic outcomes. Once we acknowledge the precarious nature of the health benefits of homeownership, then we owe it to the families we serve to ensure that the homeownership experience is successful. These findings provide a sobering reminder of the damage wrought on families who were poorly served by misguided efforts to promote homeownership with unregulated lending. Not only was indelible harm inflicted on their financial lives and their neighborhoods, but their physical and mental health were put at risk.

A Place Called Home ends with a set of policy recommendations that, if implemented, would increase the likelihood that homeowners, especially low-income and minority families, would experience the financial and non-financial benefits identified by the research as being associated with homeownership. By implication, these recommendations also reduce the odds that owners would suffer the financial, social, and psychological problems we have observed in the aftermath of the Great Recession.

In a very interesting way, this work brings us full circle in its conclusion. We embarked on an effort to answer important questions about homeownership: Can low-income households become successful homeowners? If so, can they build family wealth through the homeownership experience? Can low-income homeowners experience the same non-financial benefits that we've come to believe, albeit anecdotally, that other American homeowners do? And if so, what are the likely factors that generate these benefits? The research has answered the first three questions in the affirmative. Furthermore, it has made a major contribution by identifying two important factors that appear to be responsible for the non-financial benefits accruing to homeowners—residential stability and the sense of control experienced by the owners. By identifying and understanding *how* non-financial assets are generated by homeownership, the research concludes by identifying ways to intervene in rental markets to generate some, if not all, of these same benefits for renters.

We set out to understand, defend, and promote homeownership as a superior tenure choice for low-income families because we believed it would generate the financial and non-financial assets that we thought would play an important role in their future success. We still believe, based on the crucial role that homeownership, when "done right", plays in building financial assets for owners, that it is the preferred tenure choice for low-income and minority households who can qualify for safe, responsible, and affordable mortgages (Quercia, Freeman, & Ratcliffe 2011). Ending the book with constructive ways to "do renting right" by making it an asset-generating tenure choice for families who cannot, or choose not to, become homeowners is both unexpected and welcome. Given the turbulence of the recent foreclosure crisis, with its destruction of housing wealth and the concomitant fall in homeownership rates, particularly for low-income families and families of color, the importance of this contribution cannot be overestimated.

We believe that the research presented in *A Place Called Home* makes an important contribution to the debate about homeownership in this country by identifying how it helps improve the lives of low-income and minority families and, indirectly, the communities in which they live. We are very proud to be part of the Ford Foundation team that joined with Self-Help and Fannie Mae to enable so many families to reap the benefits of homeownership and to contribute to the path-breaking research that has documented these critical benefits. We hope that the experience of these owners, the insights gained from the research, and the recommendations offered by the research team will lead to changes in public policy and the financial system that enable many more families, especially low-income and minority households, to access these benefits through owning a place that they can call home.

Frank F. DeGiovanni, Retired. Previously, Director,
Financial Assets Unit, The Ford Foundation

George McCarthy, President and CEO, Lincoln Institute of Land Policy.
Formerly, Director, Metropolitan Opportunity, The Ford Foundation

Introduction

HOMEOWNERS HAVE LONG enjoyed certain advantages in the United States— starting with the right to vote for large property owners in the 18th century and continuing through the receipt of benefits through the tax code and the government backing of the mortgage finance system today. In fact, the U.S. government has supported homeownership so much that in 2004, about seven out of 10 American families were homeowners. This support for homeownership rests on certain assumptions and beliefs: the idea that homeownership is a way for families to build equity and save money over the long-term and that it leads to positive social outcomes such as increased civic and social participation.

However, the Great Recession triggered an important conversation around the degree to which these assumptions remain true today. While the wealth-building benefits of homeownership have been studied extensively, less attention has been paid to research on the social impacts associated with homeownership. Does it hold true that homeownership can build social capital, increase civic engagement, or improve health outcomes? Does owning a home affect a person's involvement in his or her community and, if so, how? To what degree are these and other apparent impacts simply a result of fundamental differences between homeowners and renters, such as differences in income or education? The benefits of homeownership have often been taken for granted or assumed, and have not yet been subject to the same empirical treatment as the financial benefits. These questions have deep relevance in the United States at a time when many are questioning the desirability of continuing to support homeownership. Studying them can help us consider ways to make any benefits associated with homeownership available more broadly to renters as well as owners.

Many researchers have examined the financial impacts of the Great Recession, including the high incidence of foreclosures, the extent to which risky lending and borrowing resulted in losses of homes and wealth, and the devastation of many of our communities. In contrast, this book focuses on the nonfinancial, or social, benefits that homeownership supposedly confers, even during a time of crisis. These questions have not been studied in depth due in part to data constraints and the difficulty of sorting through methodological issues such as simultaneity and selection bias (i.e., the fact that the characteristics of the people who purchase a home may be intrinsically different than those who rent and it could be that these a priori differences, and not the purchase of a home itself, explain differences in outcomes). We discuss these methodological challenges in further detail in Chapter 1. This book draws on a rich dataset and uses methods that seek to minimize selection issues in order to provide an analysis that measures the social benefits of homeownership, while building upon previous research in this area.

Ultimately, this book finds that there are, indeed, nonfinancial benefits to homeownership. Our analyses show that homeowners are more likely to vote, are more likely to get involved in neighborhood groups, enjoy higher levels of both mental and physical health, and feel more control over their lives. However, we also recognize that these and other social dimensions associated with homeownership may have unintended and negative aspects as well, such as the continued stratification of our communities on the basis of housing, income, and race and ethnicity (Dickerson 2014; McCabe 2016). Thus, the presence of the social impacts identified in this book should add to a broader debate about homeownership that considers both the positive and the negative dimensions of homeownership. This book concludes with a discussion of the way the United States might extend these positive aspects of homeownership more broadly to renters and owners alike.

In the remainder of this introduction, we provide an overview of the way that U.S. policy support for homeownership has evolved over the years. We discuss the expansion of lending under the auspices of the Community Reinvestment Act (CRA) and contrast the way CRA lending differs from the unsustainable and risky subprime products and services that caused the financial crisis. Then we describe the main arguments for and against the continued expansion of homeownership to low- and moderate-income households, examining both the great loss of housing wealth and uncertain financial returns to homeownership in the aftermath of the Great Recession and the potential social benefits of homeownership to individuals and communities. We close with a brief description of each of the chapters and the main findings.

Public Policy Support for Homeownership: A Short History

Property ownership has been a foundational element of Western political philosophy for centuries. The belief that owning property is one of a citizen's most basic rights is reflected in the country's founding documents (Locke 1689). The expectation that the preservation of natural rights, including the ownership of property, is the primary purpose of government itself continues to this day. Thus, it is not surprising that for much of our history, public policy has supported and promoted homeownership.

Policy support for homeownership has been justified by contending that homeownership has both financial and social benefits. Homeownership has long been understood as a financial tool for American families. For most households, the home is the single largest investment they hold and is often seen as a tool that can help build wealth over time. Ideally, a family's wealth increases as home equity grows with the periodic repayment of mortgage debt and the tax benefits associated with owning a home. Wealth also increases when house prices appreciate over time. Even for lower-income households who may have smaller initial investments, as long as the value of the home does not decline, the home can function as a savings vehicle, can contribute to financial security, and can even be a source of potential retirement income. Thus, homeownership has traditionally been seen as a secure way to build wealth.

Additionally, it has long been assumed that homeownership is associated with important social dimensions. Early in our history, owning one's home was seen as a civic virtue. Moral and ethical principles such as thrift, responsibility, commitment, and hard work are often seen as part and parcel of the homeownership experience (Quercia et al. 2011). For these reasons, both financial and social, the U.S. government has long supported homeownership.

The United States has primarily relied on two mechanisms to support homeownership: the tax code and the expansion of mortgage financing. Since 1913, the tax code has subsidized the home as an investment by allowing taxpayers to deduct mortgage interest and property taxes paid on their homes. Since the 1930s, the expansion of the mortgage finance system has also been used as a central mechanism to promote homeownership. Until that point, home mortgages were purely a private affair. Most mortgages had adjustable interest rates and five-year terms, and the unpaid principal was due at the end of the short term as a one-time "balloon payment." Homeowners had to refinance periodically, something that was not a problem as long as home prices continued to rise (Green & Wachter 2005).

During and after the Great Depression, the federal government put in place the elements of the modern housing finance system. As property values declined during the Depression, homeowners were unable to refinance, and a wave of foreclosures ensued. The federal government intervened forcefully. To stem the wave of foreclosures, the government created the Home Owners Loan Corporation (HOLC) in 1933, which purchased about a million foreclosed loans and refinanced them into a new type of mortgage instrument: fixed-rate, fully amortizing long-term loans. Between 1932 and 1938, the government also created the Federal Deposit Insurance Corporation (FDIC) to provide deposit insurance to minimize runs on financial institutions; the Federal Home Loan Bank system (FHLB) to make low-cost funds available to lend for housing and other economic activities; the Federal Housing Administration (FHA) to provide mortgage insurance; and the Federal National Mortgage Association (Fannie Mae) to purchase loans made by primary lenders, thus providing a secondary market outlet and enhancing market liquidity.

The work of these institutions, combined with the creation of the Veterans Administration (VA) under the GI Bill, resulted in the rapid expansion of home-ownership after World War II. Returning veterans were able to purchase a home with a VA mortgage insured by FHA, characterized by a low down payment (5% for new homes and 10% for existing homes) and a longer 30-year term. Veterans who needed a loan above the FHA cap had to rely on the emerging private insurance market. Over time, these policies created the suburban landscape characterized by tract houses, large lots, and car-centric, residential-only subdivisions that is typical in most American cities today.

The impacts of these policies on the promotion of homeownership should not be overestimated, nor should the downside of some of these policies be underestimated. After its creation in 1933, HOLC developed appraisal practices and standards that created a rating system that undervalued dense, mixed-use, and aging neighborhoods. Such practices and standards consistently undervalued center-city neighborhoods in favor of suburban development. This practice, often called "redlining," also rested on the idea that racially integrated and predominately nonwhite neighborhoods had unstable property values and thus posed higher risks to lenders (Hayden 2003). As a result, the federal government, through the HOLC and later FHA, began to advocate, promote, and preserve neighborhoods that were mostly all white (no more than 15% minority). While the FHA insured 60% of all home purchase loans that originated between 1934 and 1959, only 2% of these mortgages went to African Americans. Similarly, private institutions such as the National Association of Real Estate Boards and the Institute of Real Estate

Appraisers warned its members of the detrimental impacts of ethnic and racial integration on property values. Taken together, these officially sanctioned policies and practices of redlining by both government and private stakeholders contributed to the segregation that still characterizes many American cities today.

However, in 1948, the Supreme Court stated in *Shelley v. Kraemer* that racially restrictive covenants could not be enforced. This was followed by a number of presidential orders, the civil rights legislation enacted in the 1960s under President Lyndon Johnson, and ultimately the passage of the 1968 Fair Housing Act, which barred racial discrimination, private or public, in the sale or rental of property. Unfortunately, the legal dismantling of these policies and practices has done little to change the urban patterns that were put in motion when they were enacted.

The 1960s also saw the creation of financial institutions that increased access to capital. Fannie Mae was split into two agencies: the Government National Mortgage Association (Ginnie Mae) within the newly created Department of Housing and Urban Development to focus on FHA-backed loans, and a new Fannie Mae, now a privately held and federally charted company, to buy and sell non–government-backed mortgages in order to increase liquidity in the market. In 1970, the Federal Home Loan Mortgage Corporation (Freddie Mac) was created to provide a secondary market outlet for the savings and loan sector. Because of their federal charters, Wall Street and capital markets believed that the securities issued by Fannie Mae and Freddie Mac had the implicit backing of the federal government. These private but federally charted institutions could access capital at lower rates in the market because of this implicit guarantee, passing the lower costs to mortgage borrowers in the form of more affordable mortgage rates.

By the mid-1970s, concerns remained that access to mortgage credit was not available equally to all creditworthy Americans. In response, Congress passed the Home Mortgage Disclosure Act (HMDA) of 1975 requiring that lenders file annual, loan-level reports of the characteristics of the mortgages they make (including denials, race and income of loan applicant, and neighborhood in which the house is located). These reports, released in the years following HMDA's passage, showed clearly that lending problems persisted, which inspired the passage of the Community Reinvestment Act (CRA) in 1977. This act requires banks and thrift institutions to extend sustainable credit in an equitable manner.

Banks and thrift institutions responded by expanding their lending to low- and moderate-income borrowers and communities, particularly after the more quantitative performance measures were put in place in 1995.[1] Banks developed special mortgage lending programs that featured flexible guidelines (so-called affordable lending products). These programs often required borrowers to receive in-person homeownership education and counseling, which was believed to lessen the risk of default and enhance the sustainability of the homeownership experience. The CRA was central to the expansion of low-cost, low-risk mortgage credit to more Americans. Overall, the homeownership rate increased from 64% in 1994 to a peak of 69% in 2004 (Spader, McCue, & Herbert 2016). Increases were even higher for African American and Latino households during that period.

Nevertheless, the impacts of these changes were not felt broadly because CRA products did not have access to capital markets. The underwriting flexibility that made the CRA activity effective in expanding credit to more Americans also proved to be its main barrier to broad adoption. Lacking standardization, these community reinvestment products often did not meet the underwriting guidelines of Fannie Mae and Freddie Mac. Thus, investors considered them to be too risky for the secondary market; as a result, CRA products had relatively limited availability. It is estimated that CRA-related programs originated between 20,000 and 30,000 loans a year. (This figure represented a small fraction of the annual average of 10 million new mortgage originations over the three years prior to the onset of the Great Recession.) Banks were ultimately limited by a lack of access to the capital provided by a secondary market outlet.

Subprime Lending and the Run-up to the Great Recession

In the early 1990s, the federal government sought to increase access to capital for more households by expanding CRA. In response to several studies contending that Fannie Mae and Freddie Mac were not buying enough loans originated to low- and moderate-income and minority mortgage borrowers, Congress established numerical goals to be met by these government-sponsored enterprises (GSEs) to better serve lower-income communities. At the onset of the Great Recession, these goals were set at 50% (i.e., 50% of the loans purchased by Fannie Mae and Freddie Mac in a given year had to be loans originated to low- and moderate-income and minority borrowers). The justification for the goals in part reflected the growing popularity of subprime loans, a different type of mortgage product increasingly used by lenders to target the typical CRA applicant. Subprime loans did not meet the criteria for prime (or A-grade) loans because of their nontraditional and risky features. Investors refer to these loans as B- and C-grade loans.

Unfortunately, subprime loans gained popularity during this period and were used primarily for low- and moderate-income and minority borrowers. They allowed many households to buy or to refinance a home. These loans were risky and expensive, characterized by high upfront fees, risk-based pricing (thus costlier in the long run for low- and moderate-income borrowers), prepayment penalties, teaser rates, balloon payments, and negative amortization. As the financial crisis that began in 2008 demonstrated, subprime loans simply did not provide the sustainable credit needed by low- and moderate-income borrowers.

With few exceptions, the federal government (Fannie Mae, Freddie Mac, Ginnie Mae, and the FHA) did not back these nontraditional loans. As a result, the loans were only privately bundled into mortgage-based securities. This market grew exponentially in a decade fueled by an oversupply of capital and a thirst for higher yields among investors. Unfortunately, the promise of higher yields and short-term profits proved too much for Fannie Mae and Freddie Mac. Eventually, they began to invest in the nonprime market, purchasing loans rated as just below prime, or Alternative-A (Alt-A). They also terminated the homeownership education and counseling requirements for their community loans. The involvement of these institutions gave these lending practices legitimacy and fueled their growth even more.

Subprime lending peaked in 2006, when more than one in five loans originated were subprime. In late 2007, delinquency rates in the subprime and risky Alt-A sectors began to climb. During this period, financial institutions failed due to mounting losses, triggering a long-term contraction in the availability of credit in the United States and around the world.

In 2008, the government took Fannie Mae and Freddie Mac into conservatorship. Shortly afterwards, nine out of 10 mortgages were purchased by the GSEs or insured by the FHA. The passage of the Dodd-Frank Wall Street Reform and Consumer Protection Act in 2010 was the country's long-term response to the crisis. The comprehensive legislation promotes safety and soundness in the financial system and bans the most egregious lending practices that led to the financing crisis. It also protects consumers from abusive practices and discourages institutions from becoming "too big to fail" to avoid the need for government involvement if they were to default. Despite its breadth, one point is clear: The legislation did little to explain the way that mortgage credit for affordable homeownership should become available again. This omission reflects the tension in the ongoing debate about the role that the promotion of homeownership played in the run-up to the crisis (Quercia, Freeman, & Ratcliffe 2011).

Despite its promise, the future of the Dodd-Frank Act is uncertain. Aspects of the Act that may be changed include the reach and governance of the Consumer Financial Protection Bureau, which was created by the Act to protect consumers, and the rule that currently bars banks from making speculative investments that could boost profits but harm consumers. Changes could also be made to reduce the costs of regulatory compliance resulting from meeting Dodd-Frank requirements. Finally, new administrations could implement changes to be sure that taxpayers are not on the hook if systematically important institutions fail.

Should We Promote Affordable Homeownership?

In the aftermath of the Great Recession, the financial benefits of homeownership have come into question. Critics argue, with good evidence, that the wealth gains associated with homeownership are far from certain. Moreover, they contend that promoting and supporting homeownership may actually harm the very families that homeownership-promotion programs are intended to help. Failure to sustain homeownership can destroy wealth, ruin access to credit, force families to relocate, and devastate communities.

The concern is understandable following the burst of the house price bubble. Since 2008, about 22% of accumulated American wealth has been destroyed (Makin 2013). Much of this loss was the result of the collapse of house values and the corresponding loss of equity for those who bought close to or at the peak of the market. At the peak of the housing boom, only 49% of African American households owned their homes compared with 75% of white households, yet wealth losses have disproportionately affected minority households: net worth declined by 53% for blacks from 2005 to 2009 compared with a decline of 16% among white households. This is because home equity represents a greater share of wealth among minority households (Kochhar, Fry, & Taylor 2011). Thus, it is clear that the Great Recession had a disproportionate impact on minority households, the very households that much of federal policy was meant to target.

Citing these high default and foreclosure rates, some have concluded that the crisis was caused by lending to borrowers who typically rely on low down payments and other lending flexibilities, typically low- and moderate-income and minority borrowers. Requiring higher down payments and stellar credit histories, these people argue, will minimize the likelihood of another crisis in the future. However, such an approach would exclude many low- and moderate-income creditworthy borrowers from homeownership while failing to address the underlying cause of the mortgage finance crisis—reckless lending on the part of financial intermediaries and the bundling of problematic loans into highly rated securities (Ding, Quercia, Li, & Ratcliffe 2011).

In fact, research has shown that mortgage borrowing by low- and moderate-income and minority borrowers did not, in itself, cause the crisis. Borrowers who bought homes with properly underwritten, fixed-rate mortgages with low down payments have weathered the crisis relatively well, and the wealth created over time has been substantial (Quercia & Ratcliffe 2010). Some say that homeownership remains an important contributor to wealth creation when done right (Quercia et al. 2011; Turner & Luea 2009). These researchers have identified factors that can enhance the wealth-building aspects of buying a home, including the timing of purchase in the business cycle (Belsky & Duda 2002), the type of the mortgage product (Ding et al. 2011), the quality of the loan servicing (Stegman, Quercia, Ratcliffe, Ding, & Davis 2007), and the presence of risk-mitigating mechanisms (Quercia & Spader 2008). In contrast, others say that at times renting may be a less expensive and less risky option (Moeller & Wittkowski 2010; Riley, Ru, & Feng 2013).

The Great Recession that began in 2008 brought these still-unanswered questions to the forefront of public policy research: If the home is not guaranteed to provide a solid return on investment, is there a rationale for supporting homeownership beyond whatever financial consequences it may have? Are there social benefits to homeownership, and if so, what are they and how are they conveyed?

The Social Dimensions of Homeownership

The social dimensions associated with homeownership are contested. On the one hand, there is an idea that homeownership will lead to positive consequences for homeowners and their communities, including better health outcomes and less stress, stronger social networks and social capital, and more active participation in political (voting) and community activities. On the other hand, there is an idea that some of the same forces that lead to those positive consequences also have more detrimental impacts, such as strengthening patterns of community segregation and exclusion.

Two recent books examine these questions directly. Brian McCabe (2016) argues in *No Place Like Home: Wealth, Community, and the Politics of Homeownership* that "the core ideas about homeownership—on one hand, the importance of building wealth through housing and on the other hand, the role of ownership in strengthening communities—are not nearly as straightforward as common accounts suggest" (p. 5). He suggests that, while homeowners may indeed be more likely to vote or participate in neighborhood groups, this involvement may actually lead to segregation and exclusion. He also proposes that the important positive outcomes that do exist may be conveyed by the fact of residential stability, not by homeownership itself.

Similarly, Mechele Dickerson (2014) contends in *Homeownership and America's Financial Underclass: Flawed Premises, Broken Promises, New Prescriptions* that the legal structure around homeownership (including zoning rules, subdivision laws and policies, and also private restrictive property covenants) unfairly excludes property uses and people from certain neighborhoods. As a result, renters and others are pushed to areas with fewer opportunities. More broadly, Dickerson argues that policy must focus on making "housing—and not just homeownership—more affordable" (p. 16).

These two recent books highlight the importance of the conversation about homeownership broadly, and also point to the particular relevance of research around the social dimensions of homeownership.

While some researchers ask what impact homeownership has had on the problems of segregation, exclusion, and inequality in the United States, we ask a different question: What exactly are the positive nonfinancial, or social, benefits, however limited, that are associated with homeownership? Additionally, if some social benefits do exist, then how are they conveyed?

The literature on the nonfinancial benefits of homeownership—often referred to as the "social impacts of homeownership"—has had mixed findings. In a review of the literature, Dietz and Haurin (2003) report that several studies have found no link between homeownership and political beliefs, and others have found that homeowners are slightly more likely to vote (Kingston, Thompson, & Eichar 1984) and to get involved in local politics (Alford & Scoble 1968). Rohe and Stegman (1994b) and Forrest and Murie (1991) find that homeowners are more likely than renters to participate in neighborhood-based organizations, but this does not hold for other types of civic and community groups. Based on this evidence, Dietz and Haurin (2003) concluded that "homeownership may result in large positive social externalities, but existing empirical evidence is inadequate to support this claim" (p. 430). More recently, Engelhardt, Eriksen, Gale, and Mills (2010) found that while a simple statistical model did show a significant positive association between homeownership and voting, a sophisticated model that accounted for unobserved differences between owners and renters showed that homeowners were significantly less likely to vote in national elections.

This raises the issue of methodology, or the extent to which past findings about homeownership have been the result of methodological considerations such as "selection bias" (i.e., the idea that people who purchase a home are intrinsically different than those who rent and that it is these a priori differences, and not the purchase of a home itself, that explain differences in the outcomes). Past research on the effects of homeownership has generally struggled to account for this selection bias around homeownership. It is possible that some of the same resources that facilitate buying a home, such as having higher education, income, or wealth, also affect the outcomes with which homeownership has been associated (e.g., being in better health or being more likely to vote). The failure to control for these and other factors has led to bias in analyses comparing social outcomes for homeowners and renters (Aaronson 2000; Dietz & Haurin 2003; Rohe, Van Zandt, & McCarthy 2002). Addressing this methodological concern, this book is grounded on a decade of research on the social consequences of buying a home, summarizing evidence to shed light on the debate surrounding the social dimensions of homeownership.

Chapter Summaries

This book yields novel insights into the nonfinancial effects of affordable homeownership. It presents our findings on the social impacts of homeownership and explores not only what benefits are associated with affordable homeownership but also how and why these benefits are transferred. Unlike much of prior work in this area, we address the challenge of selection bias with a novel dataset and rigorous methodology. The dataset comes from a long-term examination of the Ford Foundation–funded Community Advantage Program (CAP), an initiative to provide a secondary market outlet for CRA loans. Under the program, Self-Help, a community development financial institution based in Durham, North Carolina, purchased community reinvestment loans from lenders and sold them to Fannie Mae, while retaining the associated risks. Between 1998 and 2009, CAP purchased over 46,000 loans made to low-income households. On an annual basis, the study collected unique household-level information from borrowers and a comparable group of renters to allow us to measure the social dimensions of homeownership on low-income families, something that had not previously been studied with a national sample of borrowers. Methodologically, the analyses in this book control for the possibility that homeowners and renters may inherently be different, something unaccounted for in most existing work on the topic.

This book is comprised of nine chapters. The majority of them assess the social consequences of homeownership, controlling for observable initial differences between owners and renters (self-selection into homeownership) in order to provide a more rigorous assessment of the interconnection between owning a home and well-being. Following these analyses of *what* benefits are associated with homeownership, we step back to ask *why* and *how* these benefits are conveyed. Finally, we discuss the implications of our analyses for public policy in a conclusion.

Chapter 1 explains the dataset and the methodology we use in our analysis. Important methodological challenges such as selection bias and simultaneity are explained. We also introduce our unique dataset, which gives us a vantage point that we use to compare homeowners with similar renters. The technique we use to make this comparison, propensity score matching and several other important methodological tools that we used to sort through issues of selection bias and simultaneity are discussed at length in this chapter.

Chapter 2 considers the relationship between homeownership and the physical health of low- and moderate-income families. Our analysis determines that homeowners have a lower risk of a physical health problem than renters. However, we also find that this association between homeownership and physical health limitations is fragile and is actually undone in the face of financial crisis: Homeowners who are financially stressed experience an exaggerated health risk compared to similar renters.

Chapter 3 examines the relationship between ownership and financial stress and financial satisfaction. We find that although homeowners were just as financially stressed as renters during the Great Recession, they were more satisfied with their overall financial situation.

In Chapter 4 we consider homeownership and mental health more broadly. Specifically, we test several hypotheses in order to understand the relationships among homeownership, sense of control, trust, and mental health problems. We explore two potential mediating factors—sense of control and sense of trust—that may explain a link between homeownership and mental health. Our analysis reveals that homeowners indeed report fewer incidents of mental health problems than renters, and we find that the sense of control that comes from ownership contributes to this positive outcome, rather than homeownership itself.

In Chapter 5 we examine one particular form of civic engagement—voting. We evaluate whether homeowners are more likely to vote in local elections than similar renters and, if so, whether the association is dependent upon specific neighborhood context. We find that homeowners who live in disadvantaged neighborhoods are more likely to vote in local elections than both homeowners in more advantaged areas *and* renters in similar neighborhoods.

In Chapter 6, we ask whether homeownership is an important factor in determining household civic engagement. This analysis provides insight into a long-running debate concerning the promotion of affordable homeownership: Does homeownership promote civic participation, or does it lock lower-income families into disadvantaged areas where they are likely to withdraw from community life?

Our analysis shows that the entry into homeownership can provide a catalyst for increasing goal-oriented types of civic engagement.

In Chapter 7, we analyze whether homeownership provides households with access to social capital via expanded social networks. We find that homeowners do have greater levels of social resources than renters, and that this relationship between homeownership and social capital remains significant even after accounting for residential stability and neighborhood characteristics.

Chapter 8 examines the links among homeownership, collective efficacy, and perceptions of crime. Prior research shows that collective efficacy, defined by both a sense of community and a willingness to solve problems, reduces violent crime in urban neighborhoods. While crime is influenced by structural factors such as poverty and unemployment, we also find that homeownership is positively associated with collective efficacy and, indirectly, negatively associated with perceiving crime as a major neighborhood problem.

Chapter 9 steps back from assessing *what* social benefits homeownership provides to examining *how* and *why* it provides them. In this chapter we consider four theoretical mechanisms that can potentially explain the homeownership effect: sense of control, residential stability, financial costs, and social identity (norms). By doing so, we start to understand why homeownership matters and begin to explore the possibility of bringing the social consequences of homeownership to the rental experience as well. The results suggest that sense of control and residential stability are associated with most of the outcomes examined, while the link between financial interest and homeownership with social outcomes is not straightforward. Furthermore, our results indicate that social identity, based around cultural norms, does not play a role in explaining any of the outcomes.

Finally, the concluding chapter of the book discusses the implications of our findings, both for housing policy and for future research. Because our work reveals how and why homeownership conveys the nonfinancial benefits associated with it, we are able to offer meaningful insight into how renting might be structured to convey those same benefits. For instance, because residential stability is a core contributor to many of the social benefits associated with homeownership, longer leases may extend these benefits to renters. Similarly, because sense of control is a contributor to some of the benefits examined, allowing renters a greater degree of control over their living environment may lead to positive outcomes.

The relationship between homeownership and positive social outcomes is a compelling topic in today's policy environment. It is crucial to understand the possible costs and benefits of homeownership as our nation moves forward to craft effective policies to support access to both owned and rental housing. We find that homeownership is, indeed, consistently associated with positive outcomes. These findings can guide our policy debates. Even more, it is our hope that this book will prove useful to academics, policymakers, and housing advocates as they strive to better understand why homeownership matters, how to extend benefits to renters, and how to make homeownership an attainable goal for all households who aspire to it.

Note

1. There were concerns that the regulatory agencies responsible for CRA examinations were more process-oriented than interested in actual results.

A PLACE CALLED HOME

1 Methods

IN THIS CHAPTER, we detail our research design, methodological challenges, analytic strategy, and data sources. These issues are covered in greater detail in associated peer-reviewed publications. We have listed these publications in the references section; therefore, we do not intend to duplicate that information here. Our goal in this chapter is to introduce the data and identify how we address the key analytic challenges to our research.

Research Design

Those who study housing in the United States have many tools available to them and ample data to consider. Many scholars have taken an historical perspective to consider, for example, housing trends over a period of decades or even centuries. We reviewed some of this history in our introduction and conveyed our view that, despite occasional setbacks, home-buying opportunities for low-income households have been enhanced over time, particularly since the policy changes that were implemented following the Great Depression of the 1930s. Scholars have already provided thorough studies of these and other historical trends in housing (Green & Wachter 2005).

Other housing scholars have used a case-study approach that focuses on just one or more neighborhoods or cities. An advantage of the case-study approach is that it provides a more comprehensive look at housing as it relates to one particular geographic area. Only through a case-study approach can we understand the local political context that uniquely affects housing decisions in various areas of the United States. The complexity of housing can often be better appreciated through careful analysis of detailed responses to open-ended interviews. Qualitative data, in particular, can be used to provide a rich and holistic understanding of how housing intersects with people's lives.

We have taken a different approach in the research for this book: Our approach is to analyze data from scientific surveys. Because we examine trends across geographic areas, our findings apply to more people than would be possible from a case study or qualitative inquiry. Thus, while our approach has limitations, it also has great strengths. Above all, it allows us to generalize our findings to the low- to moderate-income population in the United States.

In this chapter, we discuss important analytic challenges such as selectivity, simultaneity, causality, and measurement error. Then we present our strategies for addressing these challenges. Lastly, we provide details about our data source, the Community Advantage Panel Survey.

Analytic Challenges

We make an effort to address some of the critiques that have been made of earlier research on homeownership. Four major challenges come up time and again: causality, selectivity, simultaneity, and measurement error. We address each of these challenges in turn.

Concerns About Causality: Is the Homeownership Effect Real?

While examining patterns in the data, we include a variety of measures such as household income, formal education, and time in residence. In our description of models, we refer to these measures as covariates because they represent alternative explanations that could plausibly explain why homeownership is associated with social benefits. Our goal is to gauge whether homeownership remains important while acknowledging or controlling for these and other plausible explanations.

The inclusion of covariates is an effort to address some of the critiques that have been made of earlier research on homeownership. Scholars have noted that for many outcomes, the direction of causal influence of homeownership is complicated. In fact, the greatest concern is that the experience of owning a home may *not* be responsible for the associated benefits; instead, the characteristics of the people who buy homes may be the determining factor.

Individual characteristics can matter if the people who buy homes differ in important ways from those who rent; for example, if they prefer to stay in one place for a long time. When models fail to account for the possibility that owning a home is not the factor responsible for observed effects, the resulting estimates can be biased, or inaccurate. This bias can lead researchers to overstate the benefits of homeownership. It is this issue that we tackle and attempt to address in our empirical analyses.

Much of the research in this book is built on the idea of causality. In particular, our findings are based in the idea that homeownership is linked in valid ways to nonfinancial and social outcomes. By valid, we mean that cause and effect are laid out correctly.[1] A valid link requires not only a conceptual framework, but also an analytic strategy that adheres to a sensible logic of how events unfold in the real world.

Our purpose in this section is to focus on the major validity threats that we confronted in our research on the consequences of owning a home. The two major validity threats that we see, and that have been identified by other housing scholars, are selectivity and simultaneity. A third validity threat, measurement error, is a concern for all researchers that is magnified for the social outcomes that we study in this book.

The Selectivity Problem: Comparing Those Apples to These Oranges?

Studying homeownership is challenging because people do not randomly become homeowners or renters. Instead, people choose to own or rent based on their resources and preferences. The resources and preferences that influence a person's decision to own or rent are not evenly distributed in the population, nor can they be fully known by researchers.

There are, however, several elements of the homeownership decision that are knowable and measurable. For example, because a house or condominium is typically the most expensive purchase people will ever make, income is a key determinant in the decision to buy. We also know from prior research that the decision to purchase a home is closely associated with age, education, race and ethnicity, marital status, and raising children. These and other demographic factors, of course, are not randomly assigned in the population.

Together, these patterns underlying the decision to own or rent can be referred to as "selectivity." Sometimes called self-selection or selectivity bias, this phenomenon refers to the nonrandom sorting, or selection, of people into different groups. In our case, selectivity denotes the nonrandom sorting of people into the categories of homeowners and renters. The problem selectivity poses to researchers is that it can bias results.

Selectivity often occurs when a third variable, sometimes called a "confound," is related to both the outcome *and* the causal agent, which social scientists call a "treatment." For example, in the context of homeownership, a confound such as income could be related to both owning a home and having good health. The difficulty is that higher-income people are more likely both to own homes and to have better health. How, then, can we know whether it is homeownership or income that leads to good health?

If we could somehow randomly assign people to live as homeowners or renters, then we could more easily study homeownership with full confidence in the results, because with random assignment, confounds such as higher incomes would be evenly distributed across homeowners and renters. But as with many important decisions of life, it is not practical, possible, or even desirable to randomly assign people as owners or renters. Selectivity is the result of this conundrum.

To address selectivity, we use statistical methods to minimize initial differences between homeowners and renters. Essentially, before we analyze the variety of social benefits that form the major outcomes in this book, we first model the decision to own or rent. The key to our strategy is that we explicitly acknowledge and model the decision to buy or to rent.

By matching demographic and other factors between renters and owners, we address the selectivity problem statistically. For example, instead of comparing an older homeowner with a younger renter, we first match owners and renters by age, in order to match apples to oranges, metaphorically speaking. We then repeat this matching process again and again with other demographic factors. In this way, we minimize the noise of confounding variables that arises during the owner–renter decision.

Our use of statistical matching is not a perfect solution to the selectivity problem. For example, in several of our studies, we are not able to fully neutralize the differences in income between owners and renters. In such cases, we retain income as a predictor for the second-stage models of social benefits.

There is also an important limitation to the matching procedure we use most often, which is called "propensity score analysis." The limitation is that propensity score analysis does not match on what social scientists call "unobserveables"— that is, unmeasured variation that is associated with the decision to own or rent. This shortcoming characterizes all propensity score analyses that we present in this book.

The Simultaneity Problem: Putting the Cart Beside the Horse?

Another challenge to the study of homeownership has to do with the tangled directions and multiple causations that can influence the outcomes we study. Often times we think of a predictor impacting an outcome in a way that is influenced by time; not unlike the assumption that the horse always comes before the cart. But the challenge in this research is that predictors and outcomes can be simultaneous, almost as though the horse is beside the cart. Even more, sometimes the relationship goes both ways, as if the cart were actually pulling the horse. Two aspects of how bias can result from this potential "simultaneity" problem are particularly relevant to our study: reverse causality and simultaneous causation.

First, there is the possibility of reverse causality, or the idea that cause and effect flow both ways between two (or more) variables. For example, we consistently find an association between homeownership and health, and often assume that causality flows from homeownership to health. But it is also possible that good health is needed to purchase a home in the first place. More telling, good health may be needed to sustain homeownership, especially given the demands of home maintenance. In this way, health could influence the decision to own a home as well as flow from that same homeownership decision. Both factors could conceivably affect one another, which is a problem of reverse causality.

A second aspect of simultaneity bias occurs when multiple causal agents act at once. Perhaps the best example of this in our housing context concerns the potential for decisions about mobility and home buying to be jointly determined. That is, the moving location can also contribute to the home purchase decision, given the geographic variation in house prices. Particularly when moving from one housing market to another, a difference in house prices between the existing and new location can introduce simultaneity in decision making. When the costs of owning versus renting vary between locations, the decision to relocate can become entangled with the decision to buy or rent a home. Thus, in some cases, especially when people move to another area of the country, the decision to move can occur *at the same time* as the decision to buy or rent a home. When multiple factors act at once, it is difficult to sort through causality and to assign a linear link among mobility, home purchase, and location.

Measures of housing costs and neighborhood and residential stability can, to some extent, help account for this problem of simultaneous causation. Measures that combine the moving and owning decisions over time can also help account for simultaneous causation—we take such an approach in Chapter 6 on civic engagement. Specifically, we use six categories that result from combining over time the "move or stay" and "own or rent" decisions. Even more complex specifications are available that can model moving and owning decisions simultaneously and in some cases help untangle the problems of simultaneous causation.

But such models come with a price: the interpretation of results. As models become more complex, they also become more difficult to communicate in meaningful ways. Thus, we acknowledge but do not model simultaneity in this book. It is a limitation of our analyses that we do not fully address this potential for simultaneous causation, both the possibility of reverse causality and the simultaneity of decisions related to moving and owning a home. While adjusting for the simultaneity problem is an area for further research, we think most housing scholars will agree that concerns over simultaneity are secondary to those of selectivity bias in the own–rent decision, which we address throughout this book.

The Measurement Problem: Social Yardsticks?

Measurement is a core aspect of all research, and yet there is a tendency to forget that our knowledge is constrained, and even limited, by our measures. When the research topic involves commonly accepted measures, such as years or dollars, there is general agreement on how to measure these items: People may disagree on how to analyze data on dollars or years, but few dispute the measures themselves.

For many important topics in the social sciences, there is no widespread agreement on measures. Particularly with attitudinal data, measurement is challenging because the topic of interest resides not in the physical world but rather in the hearts and minds of people. However, just because these mental and emotional states are difficult to measure does not mean that they are not important. On the contrary, consider that love, happiness, depression, and empathy are among the most central features of the human condition. Such emotional states are critical to life itself yet remain challenging and difficult to measure.

Similarly, most topics in this book are difficult to measure. Mental health, social capital, civic engagement, sense of community—these are abstractions that reside in the minds of our respondents. To access these attitudes and emotions, we follow existing survey methods by asking respondents to indicate their level of agreement or disagreement with particular questions. Then, consistent with other social scientists, we assign numbers to these responses. This is certainly an imperfect approach; It is almost like using a yardstick to measure friendship or happiness.

Even our voting data, seemingly obvious and easily measured because they represent a behavior, in fact rely on the memories of our respondents and their careful attention to, and comprehension of, the wording for particular parts of survey questions (e.g., Did you vote in the *last local* election?). Furthermore, the collection of our data is susceptible to the known problem of social desirability in which survey participants respond in ways that are intended to please the interviewer or otherwise conform to societal expectations. All of these difficulties are problems of measurement, not analysis.

Given these difficulties of measurement, it is a small wonder that researchers see any variation at all. Yet we do, and the trends we observe in our data are sensible and similar to those published by other researchers. We use interview techniques, question wordings, and response options that adhere to the existing protocol of social science research. Still, it is the challenges of measurement—common to all researchers—that most complicate our understanding of the attitudinal and social aspects that we analyze in this book.

The practical implication of this challenge for readers is to exercise caution when interpreting the magnitude of effects. Generally, the direction and statistical significance of the results we report provides a good degree of confidence that an effect does exist in our data. However, the magnitude—that is, the strength of specific effects—is less certain due to the inherent difficulties of measuring social concepts. Throughout this book, we do report on the strength of the relationship between homeownership and a variety of outcomes related to health and community engagement. While we are confident in the direction and significance of effects, we ask that readers interpret their magnitudes with more caution because the aspects we investigate are difficult to measure.

"A Match Is a Match Is a Match": Our Way Forward

While we acknowledge the challenges detailed above, we also emphasize the strength of our approach. The procedures we use, particularly in matching renters to owners, are state-of-the art techniques designed for purposes such as those we undertake in this book: evaluating how the effects of homeownership compare to those of renting.

Our analytic strategy throughout the book is to neutralize those underlying differences between samples that do not directly reflect the core attributes of ownership itself. In several chapters, we directly examine whether a particular homeownership effect changes when we use different techniques to match renters to owners. We compare these effects across different matches for the same outcome, and we find that the homeownership effect has statistically consistent and substantively similar results. Therefore, at this time, we see no reason to believe that a slightly altered data-matching procedure would substantively change our findings.

Furthermore, careful readers will note that, across different outcomes and book chapters, we use a variety of related methods to address the problem of selectivity bias. That is, rather than approaching the selectivity problem with a one-size-fits-all match across all chapters, we use a number of different approaches: a treatment effects model, a bivariate probit model, a reverse longitudinal model, and several different forms of propensity score matching. We summarize these approaches by research question in Table 1.1. What is important for our readers to note is that there is strikingly little variation across the results of these various techniques.

The matching techniques we use to address the selectivity problem are effective in equalizing those measurable differences that are associated with—but not inherent to—the decision to own or rent a home. In this regard, we have highly consistent results across a wide variety of matching approaches that differ methodologically but are similar in their substantive goals. Taken together, the similarity of results across matching procedures reminds us of the words of a statistical expert whose advice we sought long ago, whom we recall saying, "A match is a match is a match." We see wisdom in these words, and we consider the convergence of results given the variety of matching procedures used in this book a strength of our analyses.

Data Source and Background

The analyses in this book rely on survey data from the Community Advantage Program (CAP), which was started in 1998 through a partnership involving the Ford Foundation, Fannie Mae, and Self-Help, a community reinvestment lender with headquarters in Durham, North Carolina. CAP was meant to expand home-purchase opportunities for low-income and minority households in the United States and would inform public policy with respect to community reinvestment lending. With underwriting capital provided to Fannie Mae by the Ford Foundation, Self-Help partnered with Fannie Mae, retaining management responsibilities while sharing financial risk. Qualifying loans were those made to borrowers who had household incomes of no more than 80% of the area median income (AMI), or were members of racial or ethnic minority groups, or were located in high-minority census tracts and had household incomes of no more than 115% of AMI.

CAP loans were originated as 30-year, fixed-rate mortgages with near-prime interest rates, and they carried no prepayment penalties or other alternative features. Based on traditional underwriting criteria, 82% of CAP borrowers would not have qualified for a prime mortgage at the time of CAP loan origination. Thus, the CAP program essentially provided prime loans to subprime borrowers.

TABLE 1.1

Data, Measures, and Research Questions

Chapter	Topic	Years of CAPS	Method to Address Selectivity of Homeowners	Research Question
2	Physical health	2009	Propensity score analysis	Is homeownership associated with a decreased risk of serious physical health problems?
3	Financial stress and satisfaction	2008 & 2009	Propensity score analysis	How did homeownership relate to financial stress and financial satisfaction during the Great Recession?
4	Mental health	2009	Propensity score analysis	Is homeownership associated with fewer mental health problems? Does trust or sense of control help explain why?
5	Local voting	2004	Instrument variable	Do homeowners vote more often in local elections? Does neighborhood context matter?
6	Civic engagement	2004 & 2007	Propensity score analysis & reverse longitudinal model	How does community involvement relate to changes in homeownership and residential mobility over a four-year period?

(continued)

TABLE 1.1

Continued

Chapter	Topic	Years of CAPS	Method to Address Selectivity of Homeowners	Research Question
7	Social capital	2007	Treatment effects & propensity score analysis	How do the overall and within-neighborhood social capital resources of homeowners compare to those of renters?
8	Collective efficacy	2006 & 2007	Propensity score analysis	How does homeownership relate to neighborhood sense of community and the willingness to fix problems? Is there a secondary link to perceptions of crime?
9	Homeownership: mechanisms and dependencies	2007 & 2008	Propensity score analysis	Do financial interests, residential stability, social identity, and perceived control help explain the effect of homeownership on health and civic engagement? Do home equity and dwelling features alter these effects?

In total, more than 46,000 loans originated between 1983 and 2010 were pur-chased by Self-Help through CAP. At the time of loan origination, the median CAP borrower was 32 years old and had an income of about $31,000 (roughly 60% of Housing and Urban Development's criteria for AMI) and a credit score of 681. The median CAP borrower received a loan of about $79,000 at an interest rate of 7% with an origination loan-to-value ratio of 97%, meaning that the loan covered 97% of the full value of the home. About 41% of CAP loans were made to female heads of household. Approximately 14% of CAP properties are located in rural areas, and about 32% are located in low-income census tracts. Nearly 70% of CAP properties are located in the South, and approximately 35% are located in North Carolina (Riley, Ru, & Quercia 2009).

The CAP loans have proven to be successful, with low overall foreclosure rates and success in terms of wealth-building for the borrowers.[2] Mortgage delinquency rates for CAP loans have consistently fallen below those for subprime loans. The median CAP borrower has accumulated about $29,000 in home equity since loan origination.

The Community Advantage Panel Survey

To facilitate an in-depth evaluation of the CAP program, the Ford Foundation funded an annual panel survey of a subset of CAP borrowers and a comparison group of similar renters. Known as the Community Advantage Panel Survey (CAPS), the data collected from these two groups provide detailed information about housing-related experiences and attitudes, as well as how these mea-sures evolved during the recent period of economic recession. The Center for Community Capital has analyzed data from this survey for over a decade, pub-lishing dozens of manuscripts that rely on this dataset, including the 2011 book *Regaining the Dream*.

The panel survey data suggest that CAP borrowers generally had a positive experience with the program. More than 86% of CAP borrowers were still owners as of 2014. In real terms, the net worth of CAP borrowers declined somewhat dur-ing the financial crisis as a result of fluctuations in asset markets, but it has mostly recovered since then. CAP borrowers generally rated their residential situations highly, and most indicated that they would likely recommend homeownership to friends or relatives.

The panel survey data also indicate that approximately 82% of the comparison group of renters intended at baseline to purchase homes in the future, while about 35% actually became homeowners during the survey period (Lindblad, Han, Yu, & Rohe 2017). Most of these new owners obtained fixed-rate mortgages and reported high levels of satisfaction with their loans, but a small percentage reported frustration with high or adjustable interest rates.

CAPS Homeowners Sample

The target population of homeowners for the CAP survey is a set of nearly 29,000 borrowers who received Self-Help loans (the Self-Help Generalization Sample) that were originated between 1998 and 2004 and met the Self-Help criteria discussed in the previous section. A subset of these borrowers were called at the beginning of the survey. From among 7,223 cases, 3,743 owners, or 52%, completed the baseline interview. Surveying continued annually, and the follow-up surveys had higher response rates that averaged about 70% through 2009, the last year of survey data analyzed in this book.

Table 1.2 presents frequencies and proportions for the group of borrowers who completed the baseline survey.[3] Slightly less than half of the respondents are female, and approximately 40% are minorities. At the time of the baseline interview, about 73% of respondents were between the ages of 18 and 40. Nearly all of the respondents (92%) were employed, and the majority (62%) were living in the South. Thirty percent of respondents had received at most a high school diploma or GED, while 25% had obtained a bachelor's degree or graduate degree. About half of the sample was living with a spouse or partner, and about half reported a household size of two members or fewer. The majority of respondents received annual incomes between $20,000 and $50,000, with only 7% making more than $50,000.

CAPS Renters Sample

The target population of the renters sample in CAPS is a set of approximately 18,640 individuals who were selected by RTI International as potential matches with the CAPS owners being surveyed, based on location and income. In particular, renters were selected from the top 30 metropolitan statistical areas represented by the owners sample and screened to be comparable to the owners with respect to an income ceiling and neighborhood proximity. In addition, individuals over the age of 65 and full-time students were excluded from the pool of eligible participants. With these additional criteria, a total of 15,943 individuals were screened and then interviewed. Approximately 10%, or a total of 1,531, completed the baseline interview and were retained for follow-up interviews. Surveying continued annually, and the follow-up surveys for renters had response rates that averaged about 75% through 2009, the last year of survey data analyzed in this book.

Table 1.2 also presents frequencies and proportions for this group of 1,531 renters. About 47% were 41 years of age or older at the time of the interview. Whites

TABLE 1.2

Community Advantage Panel Survey: Unweighted Baseline Responses

Demographic Indicators	Homeowners		Renters	
	N	%	N	%
Age 18–25 years old	709	19.0	246	16.1
26–30 years old	875	23.4	233	15.3
31–35 years old	657	17.6	175	11.5
36–40 years old	490	13.1	164	10.7
41–45 years old	359	9.6	192	12.6
46–50 years old	288	7.7	177	11.6
51–60 years old	248	6.6	221	14.5
61+ years old	116	3.1	120	7.9
Race				
White	2,292	61.2	669	43.8
Black	730	19.5	497	32.6
Hispanic	595	15.9	294	19.2
Other	126	3.4	67	4.4
Gender				
Male	2,019	53.9	453	29.6
Female	1,724	46.1	1,077	70.4
Educational attainment				
11th grade or less	328	8.8	288	18.8
High school graduate/GED	776	20.8	466	30.5
Some 2-year college	628	16.8	243	15.9
2-year degree	540	14.4	120	7.8
Some 4-year college	492	13.2	131	8.6
Bachelor's degree	567	15.2	196	12.8
Some graduate school	139	3.7	9	0.6
Graduate degree	239	6.4	62	4.0
Vocational or other license	32	0.9	15	1.0
Marital status				
Partner or companion	416	11.1	143	9.9
Married	1,714	45.8	406	28.2
Widowed	67	1.8	60	4.2
Divorced	594	15.9	309	21.4
Separated	73	2.0	90	6.3
Never married	875	23.4	433	30.0

(*continued*)

TABLE 1.2

Continued

Demographic Indicators	Homeowners		Renters	
	N	%	N	%
Household size				
1	833	22.3	501	32.7
2	1,083	28.9	398	26.0
3	761	20.3	265	17.3
4	581	15.5	211	13.8
5+	485	13.0	156	10.2
Employment status				
Working	3,456	92.3	958	62.6
Looking for work (unemployed)	120	3.2	184	12.0
Retired	63	1.7	76	5.0
Out of labor force	104	2.8	312	20.4
Geographic coverage				
Midwest	956	25.6	212	13.9
Northeast	97	2.6	0	0.0
South	2,301	61.5	1,135	74.1
West	386	10.3	184	12.0
Income				
Less than $20,000	443	11.8	777	51.7
$20,000–25,000	623	16.6	180	12.0
$25,000–30,000	676	18.1	222	14.8
$30,000–40,000	1,313	35.1	187	12.4
$40,000–50,000	446	11.9	92	6.1
$50,000+	242	6.5	46	3.1

constituted 44% of the sample, with blacks and Hispanics representing 33% and 19%, respectively. Approximately 70% of the sample was female. About half of the sample had at most a high school diploma at baseline, and approximately 17% had at least a bachelor's degree. One-third of the sample was married at baseline, while one-third had never been married, and the final third were separated, widowed, divorced, or living with an unmarried partner. Sixty-three percent of the sample was employed, and 74% were located in the South. Approximately half of the sample reported a household income of $20,000 or less at baseline, with only 3% of the sample reporting an annual income of more than $50,000.

Comparing the CAPS Sample to the Low- to Moderate-Income Population Nationwide

In this section, we compare the sample of owners who completed baseline to the May 2003 Current Population Survey (CPS) and the 2003 American Housing Survey (AHS). The CPS is a survey of 50,000 households that is conducted monthly by the U.S. Census Bureau and the Bureau of Labor Statistics. The survey is designed to be representative of the non-institutionalized civilian population in the United States, and it collects information on demographics and other household characteristics in order to provide an integrated picture of the U.S. labor force and its experiences. The AHS is a nationally representative survey of approximately 60,000 housing units that is administered by the U.S. Census Bureau every two years. The survey is designed to capture information about the characteristics of the U.S. housing stock, including housing costs and physical attributes. The survey also captures the demographic characteristics of the people who inhabit each of the targeted housing units.

To compare data patterns across surveys, we organize the CPS and the AHS data using criteria similar to that used for CAPS. We also adjust or weight the data to help correct for the bias that can result from sampling decisions and patterns of survey nonresponse. Additional details are available online (Riley et al. 2009). Our purpose here is to summarize the most important demographic patterns.

CAPS Homeowner Comparisons

Table 1.3 presents CAPS respondents at baseline in comparison to those of the CPS and AHS.[4] For homeowners, Table 1.3 shows that when compared to the CPS and AHS homeowners, CAPS homeowners were less likely to be white and more likely to be Hispanic. CAPS owners were also more likely to be male and tended to be younger, more educated, and employed. The income distribution of CAPS owners was similar to that of CPS and AHS owners, although fewer CAPS owners were in the lowest income bracket when compared with the CPS and the AHS. Across demographic comparisons, the greatest difference between CAPS owners and the CPS and AHS samples concerned geographic coverage: CAPS had very little coverage in the Northeast (3%) and over-represented the South.

CAPS Renter Comparisons

Table 1.3 also presents similar information for renters. Relative to the CPS and AHS renters, the CAPS renters were less likely to be white and more likely to be black. CAPS renters tended to be slightly older and more educated than CPS and AHS renters, more likely to be female, and more likely to be married. Employment

TABLE 1.3

Community Advantage Panel Survey Compared to Low- to Moderate-Income Population Nationwide

Demographic Indicators	Community Advantage Panel Survey (CAPS)		Current Population Survey (CPS)		American Housing Survey (AHS)	
	Home-owners	Renters	Home-owners	Renters	Home-owners	Renters
	(N = 29K)	(N = 18K)	(N = 16M)	(N = 18M)	(N = 17M)	(N = 18M)
Age						
18–25 years	18	15.6	4.1	16.8	3.1	19.4
26–30 years	22.6	16.1	6.6	15.7	6.2	14.4
31–35 years	17.8	11.8	10.4	15.6	9.4	14
36–40 years	13.9	12.8	12.6	13.9	11.3	12.8
41–45 years	9.8	12.2	14.1	11.8	13.8	11.9
46–50 years	7.9	10.8	13.2	9	13.8	9.6
50–60 years	6.9	13.7	25.2	12.9	27.7	13.7
61+ years	3.5	7	13.7	4.3	14.7	4.2
Race						
White	57.6	37.9	60.5	43.9	69.3	51.2
Black	17.6	35.7	16.2	25.2	14.6	21.8
Hispanic	21.1	22.7	16.5	23.7	10.1	18.9
Other	3.7	3.7	6.8	7.3	5.9	8.1
Gender						
Male	56.2	32.7	50.1	42.7	53.4	46.1
Female	43.8	67.3	49.2	57.3	46.6	53.9
Educational Attainment						
11th grade or less	10.3	20.4	18.7	23.4	16.7	23.1
High school graduate or GED	21.4	27.9	37.3	35.2	33.1	30
Some college/ associate degree	43.2	32.2	27.9	26.9	29.8	29.1
Bachelor's degree or higher	25.1	19.5	16.03	14.3	20.4	17.7

TABLE 1.3

Continued Demographic Indicators	Community Advantage Panel Survey (CAPS)		Current Population Survey (CPS)		American Housing Survey (AHS)	
	Home-owners	Renters	Home-owners	Renters	Home-owners	Renters
	(N = 29K)	(N = 18K)	(N = 16M)	(N = 18M)	(N = 17M)	(N = 18M)
Marital Status						
Married	53.4	33.7	49.9	28	47.2	25.1
Widowed	2.1	4	6.5	3.2	7.6	3.4
Divorced	16.8	21.9	21.2	21.09	24.3	20.9
Separated	2.1	6.6	5.5	10	4.8	10.1
Never married	25.6	33.8	16.9	38.1	16.1	40.4
Household Size						
1	21.2	31.4	27.7	37.6	28.3	37
2	27.7	25.9	26.9	19.4	30.5	24.8
3	19.8	17.3	17.1	17.5	17.1	16.4
4	16.5	13.7	15.8	14.1	13.8	12
5+	14.9	11.8	12.5	11.4	10.3	9.7
Employment Status						
Working	91.4	64.5	68.8	68.2	62.8	66.1
Looking for work/ unemployed	3.4	13.5	4.6	7.2	37.2	33.9
Retired	2	4.2	9.2	2.4	-	-
Out of labor force	3.2	17.7	17.4	22.2	-	-
Geographic Coverage						
Midwest	24.3	10.1	21.3	19.8	25.8	21
Northeast	2.8	0	15.7	19.6	17.1	19.4
South	56.3	72.4	40.2	34.9	38.3	34.4
West	16.7	17.5	22.8	26.7	18.8	25.2

(continued)

TABLE 1.3

Continued

Demographic Indicators	Community Advantage Panel Survey (CAPS)		Current Population Survey (CPS)		American Housing Survey (AHS)	
	Home-owners	Renters	Home-owners	Renters	Home-owners	Renters
	(N = 29K)	(N = 18K)	(N = 16M)	(N = 18M)	(N = 17M)	(N = 18M)
Income						
Less than $20,000	13	47.4	26.9	49.2	25.4	44.2
$20,000–25,000	16.5	11.8	13.7	12.7	10.3	12
$25,000–30,000	17.3	14.6	14.9	12.3	12.7	11
$30,000–40,000	33.7	14.4	29.4	17.5	27	19.9
$40,000–50,000	12.3	7.5	8.5	5.1	15.1	9.4
$50,000+	7.2	4.4	6.6	3.2	9.6	5.5

status was similar between CAPS renters and those of the AHS, but CAPS renters who were not working were more likely to be looking for work compared with CPS renters who were not working and were more likely to be out of the labor force. CAPS renters were more likely to be married than AHS and CPS renters and were slightly older and more educated than their counterparts in the CPS and AHS. The income and household size distributions were similar for CAPS renters compared with CPS and AHS renters. The largest discrepancy between CAPS renters and those of the CPS and AHS involved geographic coverage. Over 72% of CAPS renters were located in the South, compared with 35% of CPS renters and 34% of AHS renters. Nearly 20% of CPS and AHS renters came from the Northeast, while none of the CAPS renters did.

Overall, these comparisons indicate that the weighted CAPS samples were largely representative of low-income and minority owner and renter populations in the United States that would have potentially been eligible for CAP loans. However, CAPS participants were also somewhat more educated, more attached to the labor force, and more likely to be located in the South compared with the general low-income and minority population.

Analytic Strategy

Annual surveys are our primary source of data, and we analyze this survey data in two ways. First, we present the words of survey respondents. These are responses to open-ended questions that asked about the respondent's residential experience. Importantly, these words come from the same people who answered other questions in the survey. We display select quotes from survey respondents in sidebars throughout the book. These are not intended as qualitative inquiry; rather, our goal in showing these quotes is to help us illustrate the patterns that emerge from the second type of data we collect, the quantitative data.

Most of our quantitative data come from responses to questions with either yes/no categories or response options that fall along a continuum. For example, some items ask respondents to indicate agreement to a statement according to the following options: *strongly disagree, disagree, agree,* or *strongly agree.* Following existing survey protocol, we sometimes refer to questions that use these type of response options as "Likert-style" questions. We assign each "Likert-style" response option a corresponding number (1, 2, 3, or 4) and then average the scores across respondents. This is a standard research procedure, and all findings in our book derive from this basic method of averaging scores across survey respondents.

In this way, we identify data patterns by first aggregating responses for the several thousand people who participated in our surveys. We then examine trends in the data to gauge similarities and differences across survey respondents. We investigate drivers of these trends by specifying quantitative models that capture the relationship between outcomes and their predictors by accounting for alternative explanations. By closely examining patterns in the data, we are able to make inferences about the experiences of our survey respondents. Together, these processes form the basis of our statistical methods.

Notes

1. Many experts have detailed these potential threats to the validity of research endeavors and shown that causal pathways can be obscured throughout research process (Antonakis, Bendahan, Jacquart, & Lalive 2010; Cook & Campbell 1979).

2. About 18% of Self-Help's portfolio of CAP loans remained active as of the third quarter of 2016, and the cumulative foreclosure sale rate was about 7%. The median CAP borrower has accumulated about $46,000 in home equity, for an annualized return-on-equity of 20% since loan origination.

3. Slightly smaller sample sizes are evident in this table due to missing data. Crosstabs do not always sum to total sample size.

4. The table shows weighted proportions.

2 Physical Health Limitations and Financial Hardship

HEALTH IS ONE of the primary factors that contributes to quality of life. Given the large body of existing research linking health to housing, we explore these links while attending to the decision to own or rent the home. We consider physical health in this chapter; in later chapters we analyze mental and overall health. The potential for homeownership to influence physical health involves features of the dwelling as well as the broader neighborhood. Household factors, such as financial hardship, can also affect health outcomes. Studying the relationship between housing, financial hardship, and health can help us understand how people cope with difficult economic circumstances.

In this chapter, we consider how homeownership and financial hardship relate to physical health. First, we study whether homeownership is statistically associated with a decreased risk of a physical health problem that limits one's daily activities. Next, we consider how the experience of financial hardship relates to this same outcome. Finally, we analyze the potential for homeownership and financial hardship to influence each other; that is, if financial hardship increases the risk of experiencing a physical health problem, does this effect change depending on whether the respondent owns or rents the home?

We will start this and other chapters with a discussion of the literature, or the background of research, on each question. Then, we explain the mechanics of our analysis, including both our formal research question(s) and our methodological strategy, before presenting the results. We will conclude each chapter with a brief discussion on our findings and their implications.

Background

There is a substantial body of research concerning the association between housing and health. Researchers have identified around 600 studies published between 1985 and 2000 that document an association between the two (Fuller-Thomson, Hulchanski, & Hwang 2000). Most of these studies acknowledge that the study of "housing" includes more than just the physical structure of a house itself: It also includes the neighborhood, the surrounding community, and the local social and economic conditions (Fuller-Thomson et al. 2000). Each of these factors can affect a person's health. For instance, people living in attractive neighborhoods are more likely to spend time being active outside of their homes (Kuo, Sullivan, Coley, & Brunson 1998) and may therefore have better health outcomes. Poor housing conditions such as the presence of lead paint, asbestos, or mold are associated with an increased risk of injury and with both acute and chronic health problems (Dunn 2000). These and other studies have shown that housing, understood broadly, has a strong effect on residents' health.

This relationship between housing and health may also flow in the other direction: A person's health can affect his or her access to housing. For example, people with chronic health problems often find it difficult to obtain and sustain high-quality housing opportunities. This, in turn, can affect their access to employment, public transportation, positive neighborhood dynamics, and even health care. This cycle between housing and health has been termed the "drift hypothesis" (Kellett 1989). According to the drift hypothesis, people with poor health get sorted into lower-quality housing, which puts them at risk for further health problems. Similarly, the relationship between health and housing may reinforce itself, since people living in poor housing conditions may develop health problems that limit their opportunities to improve their housing situation. While most research focuses only on one direction of the two-way relationship between housing and health, it is important to recognize that the two can reinforce each other.[1]

There are several reasons why homeownership may be linked to better physical health. In a review of the literature on housing and health, Fuller-Thompson and colleagues (2000) found that most research on the decision to own or rent and well-being has focused on the physical dwelling and the surrounding neighbor-hood. The link between health and homeownership may be due to the physical dwelling because, when compared to renters, homeowners are more likely to live in high-quality or newer dwellings free of problems like toxins, mold and mildew, decaying or problematic infrastructure, and more. Conversely, renters are more likely to live in dwellings that expose them to health risks (Hiscock, Kearns, MacIntyre, & Ellaway 2003; Rosenbaum 1996). Thus, characteristics of the dwelling that can affect health include chemical or biological hazards, unsafe structural ele-ments, and environmental conditions such as coldness or dampness (Northridge, Sclar, & Biswas 2003). New single-family dwellings are more likely to be sold as owner-occupied units than as rental units because it is much less expensive to build rental units as attached units such as apartments or townhouses. Because renters are more likely to live in dwellings that expose them to disease or the risk of injury, they are more likely to experience the negative health consequences of such exposure.

In addition to dwelling quality, neighborhood-wide physical conditions can have an effect on health. Homeowners are more likely than renters to live in areas where there are amenities and resources that promote health, such as public spaces for recreation, which draw residents outdoors and encourage exercise (Hartig & Lawrence 2003). Homeowners are also more likely to live in more affluent neigh-borhoods that are less likely to host heavy car traffic; this increases the oppor-tunities for outdoor recreation and decreases unhealthy air quality. Additionally, homeowners are less likely to live close to undesirable land uses such as a landfill or a brownfield.

> I enjoy having a home. It is a good feeling. It does not belong to anybody, it is ours ... you don't have to give it back.

Along with the health benefits associated with dwell-ing and neighborhood quality, homeowners may benefit from a third advantage—a privileged social position. Homeownership suggests a higher social status, so much so that owning a home is often referred to in popular cul-ture as a key part of the "American Dream." Studies have found that a person's privileged social status can actu-ally improve his or her health (Abbott 2007; Macleod & Smith 2003). Thus, renters may be at greater risk for health problems because American culture places such a high value on homeown-ership and thus devalues renters.

Finally, homeowners may simply feel more "at home" in their lives. Researchers have suggested a phenomenon referred to as "ontological security," which refers to a feeling of "confidence, continuity, and trust in the world" (Hiscock et al. 2001). Several researchers have documented an association between homeownership and this type of security. One study in Scotland found that homeowners talked about their homes as a source of stability and consistency, and concluded that they felt greater autonomy than renters (Dupuis & Thorns 1998; Hiscock et al. 2001). Another study in New Zealand found similar results: Owning a home provided people with a sense of identity and a secure, consistent space to which they could return (Dupuis & Thorns 1998). As later chapters will show, this association of homeownership with a greater sense of control over one's life will turn out to be the key factor explaining health outcomes.

Additionally, research suggests that financial hardship is negatively associated with a person's health outcomes. Whether as a result of unemployment (Bartley 1994), chronic poverty (Pappas, Queen, Hadden, & Fisher 1993), or high debt (Drentea & Lavrakas 2000), people experiencing financial hardship are at greater risk of health problems.[2] Not only do they have fewer resources to draw upon in the event of a health problem, people in financial hardship may experience greater stress, which can also raise the risk of health problems.

Our analysis seeks primarily to understand the relationship between homeownership and physical health. Additionally, we consider whether financial hardship might impose challenges that actually counteract any positive health benefits from homeownership. Past studies have found that homeowners report better health than renters (Dunn 2000; Fuller-Thomson et al. 2000). However, these links between housing and health have not addressed concerns over selectivity bias; that is, the research has not fully studied whether the characteristics of the people who buy homes may be driving healthier outcomes, rather than homeownership itself.

The Analysis

In this chapter, we study three research questions. First, how does homeownership relate to physical health? Second, how does homeownership relate to financial hardship? Finally, does the relationship between financial hardship and physical health differ for homeowners and renters? The outcome that we examine in this chapter is physical health, and our analysis uses the following survey question: "During the past four weeks, were you limited in the kind of work or other regular activities you do as a result of your physical health?"[3] This item comes from the short-form health survey that was validated by Ware, Kosinski, and Keller (1996) and Jenkinson and colleagues (1997). The question is widely used by the World Health Organization and is considered a reliable single-item measure of overall physical health. The two variables of interest are homeownership and financial hardship. Homeownership is an indicator of the respondent's decision to own or rent the dwelling. As with all analyses in this book, we first model this decision to own or rent in order to address the potential for the selectivity of this decision to bias results.

Financial hardship is measured using an index composed of 12 items indicating different experiences of financial hardship. The index consists of responses to questions that ask whether the respondent did the following during the prior year: postponed paying bills, postponed routine dental visits, postponed routine doctor visits, postponed purchasing prescription medications, postponed other medical treatment, postponed home repair (for homeowners) or home purchase (for renters), borrowed money from friends or family members, delayed starting or expanding a family, reduced household expenses, increased shopping at discount stores, bounced a check, or missed credit card or loan payments.

Each item in this financial hardship index is coded 1/0 to indicate whether the respondent experienced the hardship. The 12 items in this index are summed so that a respondent experiencing all 12 hardships would have a score of 12, while one experiencing no hardships would have a score of 0. Higher scores indicate greater financial hardship.[4]

Our analysis also includes demographic variables in order to adjust or control for factors that might be related to the outcome, physical health problem. At the household level, the models adjust for age, gender, race or ethnicity, marital status, and children in the home. At the neighborhood level, the models adjust, at the level of the census tract, for percentages of single parents, households below the poverty line, families receiving public assistance, and people who are unemployed. These four measures are combined to form a single index where higher values indicate greater neighborhood disadvantage.[5] This index, called "neighborhood disadvantage," is a variation of the index put forth by Sampson and Groves (1989). To focus the presentation, in this chapter we limit the display of covariates to our research question of homeownership, financial hardship, and physical health. As with all chapters in the book, the sample is first adjusted for selectivity into owning or renting the home.

Results

Before presenting results from models, we discuss the financial hardship index. Table 2.1 displays a cross-tabulation of housing status and financial hardship. The table shows that, on the 12 items in the financial hardship index, renters were significantly more likely than homeowners to have experienced four of the financial hardship indicators: postponing dental care, postponing other medical

TABLE 2.1

Financial Hardship Scale by Housing Status

	Renters	Owners
Postponed dental visits*	42%	34%
Postponed other medical care*	18%	14%
Delayed starting/expanding family*	23%	16%
Postponed housing payment*	55%	46%
Postponed paying bills	30%	26%
Postponed doctor visits	31%	27%
Postponed prescriptions	22%	18%
Reduced household expenses	65%	61%
Increased shopping at discount stores	54%	50%
Bounced a check	15%	13%
Missed a loan payment	18%	20%
Borrowed from friends/family	28%	28%
Average financial hardship score (0–12)	3.99	3.53

N = 1,492. Items with asterisks indicate a statistically significant difference for chi-square tests between owners (n = 746) and renters (n = 746).
*Result is statistically significant ($p < 0.05$).

(non-routine) care, postponing starting or expanding a family, and postponing making a housing payment. The finding that homeowners were less likely to skip a housing payment supports the idea that homeowners are more likely than renters to divert household resources toward staying current on the housing payment. On the other hand, it may simply be that the homeowners were more likely to have sufficient resources to stay current on all their bills. Interestingly, two of the other three significant differences between homeowners and renters in the experience of financial hardship—delaying dental care and postponing non-routine medical care—concern the family's financial ability to provide some type of care. This suggests that renters are more likely than homeowners to experience financial hardship to a degree that prompts them to cut back on what many would view as essential spending. In fact, this finding is reflected in the overall financial hardship score: Renters score about half a point higher (3.99), at the mean, on the financial hardship scale compared to homeowners (3.53).

To investigate how homeownership and financial hardship relate to physical health, we present four models. Results are shown in Table 2.2. The first model tests whether there is a homeownership effect, the second incorporates financial hardship while excluding homeownership, the third combines both homeownership and financial hardship, and the fourth captures the interaction between homeownership and financial hardship.

TABLE 2.2

Physical Health Problem Regressed on Homeownership and Financial Hardship

	Model 1	Model 2	Model 3	Model 4
Homeowner	−0.04*		−0.04	−0.11*
Financial hardship score		0.02*	0.02*	0.01*
Homeowner experiencing financial hardship				0.02*

N = 1,492, following propensity score analysis matching renters to owners.

Table displays average marginal effects. Model controls for household measures of age, gender, race or ethnicity, marital status, children in the home. Model also controls for the neighborhood measure of concentrated disadvantage, as defined in the text. We omit these covariates from this table to focus the presentation.

Estimation: Logistic regression of whether respondent reports being limited by a physical health problem.

*Result is statistically significant ($p < 0.05$).

Model 1 of our analysis shows that homeownership is negatively associated with physical health problems among respondents. These results can be interpreted in terms of percentage point differences. Thus, Model 1 shows a reduction in the risk of a physical health problem of about 4 percentage points for homeowners compared to renters.

Model 2 omits the homeownership indicator in order to focus on financial hardship. The results show that financial hardship is also associated with physical health problems. For each one-point increase on the 12-point financial hardship scale, there is an associated 2 percentage point increase in the likelihood of a health problem.

Model 3 combines the prior estimations by including both financial hardship and homeownership simultaneously. These results indicate that, once financial hardship is accounted for, the homeownership variable is not significant. This change in the effect of the homeownership variable suggests that there may be a connection between homeownership and financial hardship. More specifically, the financial hardship effect on physical health may not be uniform across homeowners and renters.

To investigate this possibility, in Model 4 we multiply the homeownership indicator with the financial hardship score. Doing so creates an "interaction" variable that isolates the experience of financial hardship for homeowners.[6] Results from Model 4 indicate that this interaction of homeownership and financial hardship is statistically significant. These results indicate that homeowners who experience financial hardship have a 2 percentage point increase in their risk of a health problem, over and above the independent effects associated with either of the "main effects" for home-ownership or financial hardship.

> We just bit off more than we could chew with the remodeling needs for this house. It has been more than we were prepared for financially and physically.

This analysis provides several findings concerning the relationship among homeownership, financial hardship, and physical health. First, homeownership is associated with a reduced risk of a respondent being limited in his or her regular activities as a result of physical health. Second, financial hardship increases this risk of a physical health problem. Lastly, there is an interaction between home-ownership and financial hardship: Homeowners who are financially stressed experience an additional risk for health problems beyond the impact associated with financial hardship alone.

Conclusion

While these results give some insights about the relationship among homeowner-ship, financial hardship, and physical health, we do not make claims about causal-ity. As we discussed in the Methods chapter, many of these questions are difficult to sort through due to the challenges of measurement, selectivity, and simultane-ity. What we have done in this chapter is to adjust for the potential selectivity bias in the respondent's initial decision to own or rent a home. Thus, we better isolate a one-way homeownership effect on the outcome, physical health problems. Along the way, we introduced "main effects" and "interactions" as terms that we will con-tinue to use through the remainder of this book.

What do these findings offer to the field of housing research and how do they inform the current debates on housing policy? The importance of this analysis rests on the evidence of positive health outcomes associated with homeownership and also on the inclusion of financial hardship as an interaction, or moderating fac-tor. Although we find an association between homeownership and physical health, those homeowners who do experience financial hardship can suffer exaggerated health consequences compared to renters who experience financial hardship.

These associations hint at useful policy levers. For instance, emergency assistance for families who experience income or expense shocks can not only help families stay in their homes, but can potentially mitigate the health consequences—and associated expenses—of such shocks. For instance, the Hardest Hit Fund, a program that was initiated in the wake of the financial crisis, is meant to help homeowners who are unemployed. It is also possible that the adoption of the Patient Protection and Affordable Care Act in 2010 may have ameliorated some of the negative impacts of health-related financial crisis for low- and moderate-income homeowners, although future research will need to study this possibility.

This chapter explored the relationship between homeownership and physical health while also introducing a third factor into the analysis: financial hardship. Our findings indicate that homeownership is associated with a reduced risk of physical health problems, but also that this positive result for homeownership is fragile and may actually be undone in the case of financial hardship. In our next chapter, we build on this conversation and explore respondents' stress in context of the financial crisis.

Notes

1. Because causality may flow in both directions, these potential links between housing and health provide a good example of the reverse causality concern that we discussed in the prior chapter about methods. We acknowledge this concern, as noted, yet in this book we focus on what we see as a more pressing threat to the validity of a potential homeownership effect: the selectivity of the decision to own or rent. We address this primary concern, selectivity bias, by matching renters to owners.

2. It is important to note that many of the studies discussed here relied on data collected prior to the housing market downturn and Great Recession, which could have altered the homeownership experience.

3. The measure is coded 1/0, and "don't know" and "refused" responses are recoded as missing data.

4. These items have a reliability coefficient of 0.79.

5. To create this "neighborhood disadvantage" indicator, we first transform the percentages to z-scores so that the items are comparable. We then sum the four items. We then divide by four, which is the number of items in the index. Among our survey participants, this neighborhood disadvantage score ranges from –1 to 6.26, with a mean of close to zero.

6. Following existing research protocol, we refer to the original variables (homeownership and financial hardship) as the "main effects," and we refer to their combination or product as an "interaction."

3 Financial Stress and Satisfaction

IN THE PREVIOUS chapter, we studied the connection among homeownership, financial hardship, and physical health. Our analysis suggested that while homeownership is associated with a reduced risk of physical health problems, the experience of financial hardship can undo and counteract that important benefit. This chapter takes up the issue of how the financial attitudes of homeowners and renters compare to each other. With CAPS data, we examine financial attitudes during the Great Recession, one of the most dramatic macroeconomic periods in generations.

In this chapter, we build on our previous analysis in order to examine homeownership for low- and moderate-income households in the context of the financial crisis of 2008. Given that the financial crisis was rooted in housing and risky mortgage lending, leading to house price declines and home foreclosures nationwide, it is possible that the financial stress associated with these events was greater for homeowners when compared to similar renters. This analysis asks: Was financial stress or satisfaction reported differently by homeowners than by renters? More broadly, how do the financial attitudes of homeowners and renters compare during times of economic turmoil? To answer these questions, we investigate the intersection of homeownership status, economic conditions, and two dimensions of financial attitudes: stress and satisfaction. We focus this analysis specifically on the time period during the housing market downturn at the height of the Great Recession.

Background

This chapter analyzes whether financial stress and financial satisfaction are factors that may be connected to the homeownership experience. In this section, we review the literature around financial security and homeownership before developing the connection among financial attitudes and homeownership. Following this discussion of previous research, we turn to our analysis.

> Owning a home helps with taxes, helps with the credit report, gives me a sense of ownership and a place to call home. It is better than paying someone else's mortgage.

Although it has been questioned since the financial crisis, research indicates that low- and moderate-income households can build wealth as a result of homeownership. Herbert and Belsky (2008) reviewed the research on the costs and benefits of homeownership for low-income and minority households and found that, overall, they are as likely to realize financial benefits as are others. However, this finding came with the caveat that households with fewer resources have a more tenuous hold on homeownership. The authors concluded that the wealth-building potential of homeownership is sensitive to a number of factors, including the length of time spent in homeownership versus renting, the level of rents relative to home prices, house price changes, timing of purchase, location, and terms of financing. As long as house prices increase, homeownership remains a viable wealth-building prospect. However, highly leveraged households can quickly lose both their accumulated equity and original investment when house prices decline.

Santiago and colleagues (2010) analyzed lower-income households that purchased homes through an asset-building program in Denver and found that households with incomes at or below 50% of area median income (AMI) generally experienced equity gains and wealth accumulation through homeownership. However, they also found that the lack of access to resources that can be turned quickly into cash put these households at greater risk of accumulating debt and experiencing mortgage delinquency. Furthermore, they noted that all the home-buyers in their study received very favorable mortgage terms and extensive pre-purchase counseling. It is likely that lower-income home buyers without these advantages experience a greater risk of financial hardship as a result of home-ownership. This suggests that homeownership is not guaranteed to be the most financially advantageous choice for low-income households, but, when accompanied by sustainable mortgages, is likely to be associated with financial gains.

Similarly, other researchers have found that homeownership can be risky as a wealth-building mechanism for low- and moderate-income households. For instance, research has shown that housing represents a greater share of the wealth of lower-income households than it does for higher-income households (Bucks, Kennickell, Mach, & Moore 2009). Thus, a fall in U.S. house prices, such as that which occurred after the collapse of the housing market, has the potential to ravage the wealth of families whose assets are most concentrated in their homes. Additionally, when housing markets boom, price appreciation can have a negative effect on affordability, driving up the price of housing. This can put home purchase beyond the reach of lower-income families. In 2008, among working households earning 50% to 80% of AMI, 32% of owners paid more than half of their income toward housing costs, while only 7% of renters paid this much (Waldrip 2009). Some researchers conclude that, due to the financial challenges of homeownership, renting may at times be a better option (Moeller & Wittkowski 2010; Riley, Ru, & Feng 2013).

> With the uncertainty of the future and the economy, it's good to not own a home so you can pick up and move for a job.

Thus, prior research indicates that low- and moderate-income homeowners are especially vulnerable during economic crises, which can put their wealth at risk or transform homeownership into a burdensome commitment. There is a belief that some of this risk could be mitigated through homeownership counseling and education, since better-informed households may make better financial decisions even in the face of challenging economic circumstances (Collins & O'Rourke 2010; Quercia & Spader 2008).

> My homeownership experience has all been good, it is just with the mortgage crisis that I did not expect to stay in the house this long because the overall market is bad.

There is also research that suggests that renting can, in certain circumstances, be more financially advantageous than owning for low- and moderate-income households. To estimate the relative wealth-building effects of homeownership, Bostic and Lee (2009) simulated the wealth-accumulation effects for low-income owner and renter households for 72 combinations of household types, mortgage instruments, neighborhoods, appreciation rates, and time horizons. In most scenarios, homeowners came out ahead. In some scenarios, however, renting did lead to a better outcome financially, particularly when low-income households purchased homes in middle-income neighborhoods and in low-appreciation markets with down payments of 5% or less.[1] Again, these results underscore the fact that home-ownership can, in normal circumstances, be an important wealth-building mechanism for low- and moderate-income families, but this result is not guaranteed.

Aside from potential financial benefits, some researchers have also discussed the connection between homeownership and psychological health. Although the literature on the psychological benefits of homeownership is less developed than that of the financial benefits, it suggests that such a link may exist. Most of this research has been conducted during times of appreciating housing markets. However, since the financial crisis, a number of studies have documented negative psychological consequences related to mortgage delinquency and home foreclosure (Rohe & Lindblad 2014).

Research before the financial crisis indicates that low-income owners generally report feeling more satisfied with their homes and neighborhoods than renters do, and report nearly the same level of life satisfaction as owners do overall (Herbert & Belsky 2008). Studies of low-income owners and renters in Baltimore (Rohe & Basolo 1997; Rohe & Stegman 1994a) found mixed evidence regarding the psychological impacts of homeownership. The studies found no effect on homeowners' perceived control over life three years after buying. However, homeownership was correlated with improved self-esteem indirectly as a result of better housing conditions and was strongly associated with increased overall life satisfaction. Thus, although the research is not conclusive, evidence suggests that homeownership can have an impact on an individual's psychological well-being.

> Because of the mortgage crisis, I can't sell this place. I have two empty houses behind me ... now I can't sell my house.

The connection between experiences of financial stress and financial satisfaction has not been fully explored within the realm of housing research, though research is beginning to provide some insight into homeowners' experiences of the financial crisis overall. A 2010 National Housing Survey by Fannie Mae found that approximately 38% of respondents felt stressed about their ability to pay debts, with a much greater share of renters (46%) than owners (25%) feeling somewhat or very stressed. Interestingly, renters were less pessimistic about their personal financial prospects than owners, with 11% of renters and 23% of owners anticipating deterioration in their family's financial situation. This survey seems to corroborate earlier research findings: Homeowners may experience a higher level of stress about their debt than renters in times of economic crisis, but may nevertheless feel less stressed about their long-term financial situation.

Despite this preliminary work, the connection between the economic dimensions of homeownership and the psychological experiences of it is not clear. Our analysis aims to help clarify this relationship by examining the linkages between housing status and the psychological and financial stress experienced by low-income households. This question matters because we are curious about whether homeownership can exacerbate financial stress during economic downturns. If owning a home during challenging economic times causes stress, it can raise questions about the promotion of homeownership as a policy goal. For these reasons, we investigate whether homeownership was associated with an increase in financial stress and financial satisfaction during the Great Recession.

The Analysis

This analysis investigates how financial stress and satisfaction relate to home-ownership, using data from 2008–2009, the peak years of the financial crisis. Homeownership status and the demographic background of the respondents were measured in 2008, while the outcomes, financial stress and financial satisfaction, were measured in 2009. As with other chapters in this book, we address the selectivity of the decision to own or rent by matching renters to homeowners. However, what distinguishes this chapter from all others in this book is that we showcase several different ways to perform this match. Before discussing these techniques, we detail key measures in this study.

The two dependent variables are level of financial stress and level of financial satisfaction. The *financial stress* measure combines six survey items that ask respondents about their finances. Four of these items measure financial stress, with response options coded as follows: 0 for "not at all stressful," 1 for "somewhat stressful," and 2 for "very stressful." Using this scale, respondents indicated how stressful they found each of the following four things: paying their rent or mortgage, maintaining their dwelling, managing money, and saving for retirement. For the other two items, respondents rated their agreement as "not at all true" (coded 0), "somewhat true" (coded 1), or "very true" (coded 2). Using these response options, respondents indicated agreement with the following questions: How true is it that you pay too much rent or mortgage? How true is it that you have too much debt? Response options for all six of these items were summed, and the scale ranges from 0 to 12. Respondents averaged 3.64 on this *financial stress* score.[2]

The second dependent variable, *financial satisfaction*, is a single-item indicator that provides a general measure of satisfaction with one's financial situation. We measure financial satisfaction using the following question: "How satisfied are you with your overall financial situation?" The response options were coded as follows: 1 for "not at all satisfied," 2 for "somewhat satisfied," and 3 for "very satisfied." Respondents averaged 1.74 on this three-point measure of *financial satisfaction*.

Our key independent variable is homeownership, a measure we hold constant between 2008 and 2009; that is, we exclude households that switched homeownership status between 2008 and 2009. We address the potential for selectivity bias in the decision to own or rent with four matching techniques. There are a variety of ways to match data between groups, and all methods rely on the same basic principle of equalizing differences between the groups being compared. Thus, the distinctions between these methods concern the details of how the observations are matched. It is always possible that a different match could yield different results; therefore, our analysis considers four different matching models, each of which selects observations according to a slightly different formula.[3] If the findings, particularly for homeownership status, are consistent across all the different matching algorithms, it will provide evidence that the findings are robust and reliable.

In addition, we show estimates for three measures of household finances: income, reduction in income, and unexpected expenses. Household income is measured as it relates to the local cost of living by representing it as a percentage of the AMI, and we call this measure *relative income*.[4] A second measure is reduction of income in the past year; about 44% of households in the analytic sample experienced a reduction of household income during the study period. Third, 35% of the sample reported experiencing a major unexpected expense in the past year. Finally, the models also adjust for additional variables, including age, net worth, region, and sense of control. We also include additional covariates in the first-stage models matching renters and owners in order to optimize the match, as described more fully in Chapter 1. However, to focus the presentation these also are excluded from the tables presented for this chapter.

The overall goal of our analysis is twofold: (1) to assess how homeownership relates to financial stress and financial satisfaction and (2) to determine whether any observed homeownership effect is consistent across different matching techniques. As noted, we match renters to owners in several different ways in order to see whether results are consistent.

Results

We analyze financial stress and financial satisfaction with four different techniques that match renters to homeowners. Each match has the same goal of minimizing the differences between homeowners and renters that are associated with, but not inherent to, the decision to own or rent a home.[5] In this way, we better isolate the effect of homeownership itself. The results, presented next, are consistent across all four techniques. This consistency in results gives confidence that the techniques we use to match renters to owners provide robust and reliable estimates of the homeownership effect.

TABLE 3.1

Financial Stress Regressed on Homeownership Matched to Renting in Four Ways

	Match 1	Match 2	Match 3	Match 4
Homeownership	−0.24	−0.19	−0.23	−0.18
Relative income	0.21	0.12	0.10	0.13
Reduction in income	0.23	0.19	0.17	0.19
Unexpected expense	0.52*	0.35*	0.35*	0.36*

The table displays coefficients from four different techniques that match renters to homeowners—in order to minimize selectivity bias of the respondent's decision to own or rent the home—as follows: Match 1 ($N = 1,234$) is a within-caliper match, Match 2 ($N = 3,078$) is a weighted propensity score, Match 3 ($N = 2,578$) uses coarsened exact matching, and Match 4 ($N = 2,987$) is an instrumental variable model. Model specification controls for respondent age, net worth, region, and sense of control, which is defined in later chapters. We omit these variables from this table to focus the presentation.

Estimation: Linear regression of financial stress index.

*Result is statistically significant ($p < 0.05$).

As for the two outcomes, Table 3.1 indicates that homeownership is *not* statistically associated with financial stress in any of the four matches. This finding indicates that homeownership during the 2008–2009 study period—when compared to renting—did not financially stress respondents. Two other variables, household income and income reduction in the past year, are also not statistically significant. However, one variable is statistically significant across all matches: Experiencing an unexpected major expense in 2008 is associated with higher levels of financial stress in 2009.

The second outcome, *financial satisfaction*, also provides consistent results across the four matches. Results are displayed in Table 3.2 as odds ratios from an ordinal logistic regression. This financial satisfaction outcome is a single-item indicator meant to capture how the respondent feels about his or her financial situation; higher values signify greater financial satisfaction. For the odds ratios, values above 1 indicate a higher likelihood of satisfaction; thus, homeownership is positively associated with financial satisfaction across all four matches. This consistent result indicates that, during the 2008–2009 study period, homeowners expressed higher overall financial satisfaction than similar renters. Note that estimates of household income and the presence or absence of unexpected major expenses are not associated with financial satisfaction. However, income reduction in the past year is statistically significant. With odds ratios below 1, these results indicate that a reduction in household income in the past year is associated with a decrease in the financial satisfaction indicator. This finding indicates that income shocks are linked to a reduction in overall financial satisfaction.

TABLE 3.2

Financial Satisfaction Regressed on Homeownership Matched to Renting
in Four Ways

	Match 1	Match 2	Match 3	Match 4
Homeownership	1.37*	1.27*	1.31*	0.07*
Relative income	0.85	0.94	0.93	−0.02
Reduction in income	0.80	0.83*	0.84*	−0.05*
Unexpected expense	0.87	0.92	0.91	−0.03

The table displays odds ratios from four different techniques that match renters to homeowners—in order to minimize selectivity bias of the respondent's decision to own or rent the home—as follows: Match 1 ($N = 1,234$) is a within-caliper match, Match 2 ($N = 3,078$) is a weighted propensity score, Match 3 ($N = 2,578$) uses coarsened exact matching, and Match 4 ($N = 2,987$) is an instrumental variable model. Model specification controls for respondent age, net worth, region, and sense of control, which is defined in later chapters. We omit these variables from this table to focus the presentation.
Estimation: Ordinal logistic regression of financial stress index.
*Result is statistically significant ($p < 0.05$).

We find evidence that even during the Great Recession, homeowners were more likely to feel greater satisfaction with their overall financial situations. However, the level of financial stress felt during this time was similar for homeowners and renters. These findings are consistent across several different methods that we use to statistically adjust for selectivity in the decision to own or rent the home.

Conclusion

> Homeownership makes you keep a handle on your finances. It gives you pride, responsibility, a sense of being.

This chapter serves two purposes, one methodological and the other conceptual. The methodological contribution is to investigate whether different ways of matching renters to homeowners would yield similar results for a potential homeownership effect. Using four different statistical techniques to match renters to homeowners, we find consistent estimates for homeownership status across the matches. For the first outcome, the financial stress scale, all four matches indicate a null finding—that is, homeownership is *not* associated with financial stress. For the second outcome, financial satisfaction, all four matches point to a consistent effect for homeownership status—that is, homeownership is *positively* associated with higher financial satisfaction. These results demonstrate that, regardless of the technique we used to match renters to homeowners, consistent results were obtained. This consistency provides confidence that results related to the home-ownership effect are robust and do not reflect the peculiarities of a particular matching technique.

The consistency of these findings across matches lends support to the second contribution of this chapter, which is more conceptual. Substantively, the findings in this chapter contribute to our understanding of the effects of homeownership by demonstrating a resiliency among homeowners during the financial turbulence of the Great Recession. Not only was the Great Recession the most severe macroeco-nomic shock in decades, but it was, in fact, directly connected to housing through unsustainable mortgage lending. Despite this, the homeowners we studied were remarkably resilient, experiencing levels of financial stress that were comparable to those of similar renters. Furthermore, these homeowners were actually more satisfied with their overall financial situation than comparable renters.

The fact that lower-income homeowners and renters experienced similar finan-cial stress during this period, yet the homeowners reported significantly higher levels of financial satisfaction, suggests that the benefits of homeownership may extend beyond household economics. While homeownership did not lessen the financial stress associated with the financial crisis, it did not exacerbate that stress either. Overall, our findings suggest that homeownership may carry with it intan-gible benefits, namely a greater overall sense of financial satisfaction. In our next chapter, we consider whether this attribute of homeownership is connected to broader mental health benefits.

Notes

1. As the authors point out, their simulations rely on stylized assumptions about household behavior and do not necessarily reflect actual outcomes.

2. The Cronbach's alpha for the financial stress scale is 0.75. The standard deviation is 2.76.

3. The details of these matches are shown in Manturuk, Riley, and Ratcliffe (2012).

4. Relative income is a measure that captures regional differences in the cost of living; it is calculated as the ratio of household income to AMI at the metropolitan statistical area level.

5. The four matching techniques that we use to address the selectivity problem each provide a slightly different strategy to minimize the impact of potential homeownership confounds such as income, age, and education level. Matches 1, 2, and 3 are propensity score models that adjust for selectivity only on *observed* variables—that is, the variables in the propensity score model. Match 4 uses an "instrumental variable" to account for selectivity on *unobserved* variables. All four of the matches provide consistent results.

4 Mental Health and Sense of Control

AFTER FINDING THAT homeownership is associated with fewer physical health problems and greater financial satisfaction, we move into a discussion about mental health outcomes more broadly. Since the Great Recession, homeowners have lost over $7 billion in housing wealth (Federal Reserve Flow of Funds Report 2010), and some research has found suggestive associations between homeowners who are facing foreclosure or experiencing negative equity and a greater risk for depression, chronic health problems, and undertaking risky behaviors such as smoking and drug use (Bennett, Scharoun-Lee, & Tucker-Seeley 2009). In this chapter, we examine the relationship between homeownership and mental health.

Existing research has considered the relationship between homeownership and outcomes related to mental health, such as self-esteem and life satisfaction, but the findings have been mixed (Rohe & Basolo 1997; Rohe & Stegman 1994a; Rossi & Weber 1996). Additionally, researchers have generally failed to examine the potential mechanisms that associate homeownership with mental health. For example, homeowners may experience fewer mental health problems because they are less likely than renters to live in crowded, multifamily buildings that exacerbate problems like anxiety, making the link to mental health more closely related to dwelling type than homeownership itself. In this chapter, we control for dwelling type while testing two potential mediating effects that may explain a link between homeownership and mental health: control and trust.

Our first research question has to do with whether or not homeownership reduces the risk of mental health problems. We also ask a second question: Why does homeownership reduce the risk of mental health problems? We investigate two possibilities: perceptions of being in control of the important aspects of one's life, and a sense of trust in one's neighbors. We hypothesize that these two byproducts of homeownership, sense of control and trust in neighbors, may be the reason that homeowners are less likely to experience mental health problems. By analyzing these two characteristics, we can better understand the link between homeownership and mental health.

Background

Research on the sociology of mental health has presented evidence to suggest that external social factors can play a role in one's risk of experiencing mental health problems. Much of this research has been considered at the neighborhood level; in particular, sociologists have advanced the idea that some neighborhoods are more advantaged than others. People who live in disadvantaged neighborhoods with little stability and shared trust are at a greater risk of experiencing mental health impairments (Roach & Gursslin 1965; Sampson, Morenoff, & Gannon-Rowley 2002). However, even within the most disadvantaged communities there is great variation in outcomes, and it is unclear which factors serve to reduce the risk of mental health difficulties for some residents. In this analysis, we draw on social disorganization theory, which emphasizes the importance of place, to derive hypotheses about the relationship between homeownership and mental health outcomes in low- and moderate-income urban neighborhoods (Sampson 1991; Sampson & Groves 1989; Sampson & Raudenbush 1999). This emphasis on the variation within neighborhoods highlights the importance of understanding how diverse outcomes can emerge from similar neighborhood contexts.

Research on the relationship between homeownership and mental health draws from two different levels of analysis: the individual and the neighborhood or community at large. This section details the literature on both levels, while also introducing relevant concepts like social disorganization theory, place attachment, and residential stability. Finally, we discuss existing research on the topics of control and trust—the two confounds that we explore in our analysis.

Social disorganization theory has been used widely to explore community-level differences in crime and delinquency (Sampson & Groves 1989; Shaw & McKay 1942). Originally proposed by Shaw and McKay in 1942, social disorganization theory posits that the instability and economic deprivation characterizing disadvantaged urban neighborhoods ultimately results in an inability to solve shared problems or accomplish common goals. This lack of capacity, in turn, causes increases in crime. This theoretical model has been supported across a variety of settings, including public housing projects (Roncek, Bell, & Francik 1981), neighborhoods in Chicago (Sampson & Groves 1989; Sampson & Raudenbush 1999), and rural communities (Lee & Bartkowski 2004).

Since its formulation, social disorganization theory has also been used to explain other outcomes, such as adverse health effects and lower levels of social capital. In research examining child development, Sampson (1991) found that children who lived in neighborhoods with high levels of disorder were at greater risk of experiencing health problems. Sampson also proposed that community instability matters because it prevents the development of social capital—the shared sense of trust and support for common goals that underlies cohesive and efficacious communities. Without social capital, it becomes difficult for communities to maintain social controls and reinforce pro-social behavior, whether it be refraining from crime or obtaining medical care for a child (Bursik 1988; Kornhauser 1978; Sampson 1988).

There have been several attempts to link social disorganization with mental health outcomes. Latkin and Curry (2003) found that people who thought their neighborhoods had problems with crime were more likely to experience an increase in symptoms of depression. Ross (2000) found that the increase in depression associated with poverty was entirely mediated by perceptions of neighborhood disorder. Other researchers have linked perceptions of neighborhood instability to feeling a lack of control (Geis & Ross 1998) and to mistrusting others (Ross, Mirowsky, & Pribesh 2001). In this analysis, we examine whether homeownership is linked to trust in neighbors and sense of control.

Residential instability is a key component of social disorganization theory. Institutions of control and regulation are difficult to maintain when people are not committed to remaining in a given community (Kornhauser 1978). Residents who do not expect to remain in an area very long have few incentives to devote resources toward community institutions, since they would not benefit from the institutions over the long term. Relationships, likewise, are not as durable when people expect to be leaving a neighborhood (Berry & Kasarda 1977). Thus, because homeownership is associated with residential stability, homeowners may feel more motivated to form social ties with their neighbors, since they anticipate staying put for a considerable period of time.

Prior research has shown that homeowners are much less mobile than renters: One study found that the median length of time a household stayed in any given dwelling was 2.5 years for renters but 13 years for homeowners (Anily, Hornick, & Israeli 1999). Research has also found that long-term renters and homeowners shared similarly favorable assessments of their neighborhoods (Rohe & Stegman 1994b). One study of homeowners in the Midwest found that people became more satisfied with their neighborhoods the longer they lived in them (Galster 1987). It is possible that homeowners build relationships based on their stability, and these relationships lead them to feel more trusting of their neighbors.

Place attachment, a related concept, is another factor that is likely generating homeowners' favorable perceptions of their neighborhoods and neighbors. Owning a home means owning part of a neighborhood. Brown, Perkins, and Brown (2003) refer to this as "place attachment"—a sense of ownership and commitment to the home and those in the immediate neighborhood. Overall, place attachment is stronger for homeowners and long-term renters than for more transient residents. Woldoff (2002) found that the strongest predictor of place attachment was homeownership; it was even more influential than the actual attributes of the neighborhood. Thus, homeownership creates a strong attachment to one's home and neighborhood, leading to more favorable perceptions of the neighborhood. In addition to residential stability, place attachment may also generate feelings of trust toward one's neighbors.

> It's nice to be in your own home and know that you are in a place that offers security, serenity, and quiet.

> Homeownership changed my life and makes me feel grounded. I never grew up in an owned home, and now mine is my sanctuary. I love my home!

Several previous studies have considered whether neighborhood outcomes such as crime, civic engagement, and trust are associated with an area's homeownership rate. Glaeser and Sacerdote (2000) found that the prevalence of crime declined as the homeownership rate within a neighborhood increased. Similarly, Dietz (2003) found an association between neighborhood homeownership rates and several types of civic engagement. These studies suggest that there may be something about homeownership that connects people to a neighborhood and, in turn, increases their sense of trust in their neighbors.

Empirical evidence surrounding homeownership and trust is inconclusive. Some researchers have found evidence that homeownership status actually decreases individual perceptions of trust. Rothwell (2010) analyzed data from the General Social Survey and found that homeowners were more likely than renters to report feeling that they could not trust people in general. Looking more directly at relationships with neighbors, however, Oh (2004) found that within urban neighborhoods, homeowners interacted more with their neighbors and reported trusting their neighbors more. Work by Carson, Chappell, and Dujela (2010) illustrates how individual homeownership status can affect perceptions of one's neighbors. Using qualitative data collected within one neighborhood, they found that homeowners and neighborhood leaders often talked about renters as being transient residents who would be unlikely to form social ties with others or contribute to the neighborhood. When they conducted statistical analyses of survey data from the same neighborhood, however, they found less support for this idea. Homeowners were more likely to form emotional bonds with their neighbors, but compared to other factors, homeownership status had little explanatory power in the formation of these emotional bonds. Thus, the evidence is mixed on the relationship between homeownership and perceptions of trust, and further study is needed.

A second mechanism that may mediate the relationship between homeownership and mental health is a person's sense of control. Rohe and Basolo (1997) write that sense of control is defined as a person's belief that he or she is "largely in command of important life events." In much the same way that social disorganization erodes trust within a community, it may also diminish residents' sense of being in control of their lives. Conversely, people who live in neighborhoods with low crime rates and strong social ties are more likely to feel empowered to direct the important aspects of their lives (Furstenberg & Hughes 1995). Researchers have connected this sense of control with two primary causes: increased actual control and social status.

> Everyone should have this experience. It's nice coming home to something that's yours.

Some researchers observe that homeownership itself increases an owner's level of *actual* control. Rohe, Van Zandt, and McCarthy (2002) theorize that homeowners have higher self-efficacy, or a higher sense that they can accomplish their goals, than renters because they have more actual control over the physical structure they live in—for example, homeowners can paint or renovate their homes on their own schedules, whereas many renters lack similar control over their spaces. Rohe, Van Zandt, and McCarthy (2002) also note that homeowners have more certainty about their housing costs than similar renters, who must renew their leases frequently. This is particularly true for homeowners who finance their home with fixed-rate mortgages rather than adjustable-rate mortgages. Given this higher certainty about housing costs, homeowners have more control over if and when they move from the property. In these ways, the actual control over one's living space and homeownership status may lead to a more generalized sense of control over important life events (Rohe & Basolo 1997).

Other researchers have suggested that homeowners might feel a heightened sense of control because of a broader cultural narrative about homeownership. Owning a home has long been a goal of the majority of Americans and, rightly or wrongly, has been viewed as a symbol that one has achieved financial security or social status (Doling & Stafford 1989; Perin 1977). Some research findings suggest that people who become homeowners experience higher self-esteem and a greater sense of control over their lives due to accomplishing the goal of purchasing a home (Rossi and Weber 1996). Having successfully completed the arduous task of purchasing a home, homeowners may also feel more empowered to then take on other important and difficult tasks.

Contrary to these ideas, some empirical work has found no correlation between homeownership and perceived control. Rohe and Stegman (1994a) found that women who purchased homes through a subsidy program in Baltimore reported no increase in their sense of control in the year after they became homeowners. Rohe and Basolo (1997) analyzed the same sample after three years and again found no significant relationship between homeownership and sense of control. It is not clear whether this finding represents a generalizable conclusion, yet it suggests that the link between homeownership and sense of control must be tested rather than assumed. In our analysis, we set out to test this relationship in order to understand whether a sense of control is conveyed through homeownership and, if so, why.

The Analysis

In this section, we introduce our expectations and detail some of the working definitions used in our analysis. We use data collected in 2009, after the housing market downturn began, to examine the relationship between homeownership and mental health. The goal of this analysis is twofold. First, we aim to contribute to a general theory of homeownership by moving toward an understanding of whether as well as why homeownership may be related to mental health. Second, we examine two potential mechanisms—trust in neighbors and sense of control—that may mediate this relationship.

Our expectations about the findings draw from social disorganization theory. Our first two expectations are that homeowners will report a greater sense of control over their lives than renters and that homeowners will be more likely to feel that they can trust their neighbors. Our next two expectations are that people who feel a greater sense of control over their lives will be less likely to experience mental health difficulties and that people who feel that they can trust their neighbors will be less likely to experience mental health difficulties. If these four expectations are confirmed, then the final focus of our analysis will be to examine the extent to which the relationship between homeownership and mental health is mediated by either sense of control or trust in neighbors.

Thus, we expect homeownership to have an indirect effect on mental health, with the effect mediated by sense of control and trust in neighbors. Whether this mediation of homeownership is partial or total is something we also investigate. Taken together, these ideas suggest that it is not homeownership *itself* that causes mental health but, rather, that sense of control and trust may actually convey this benefit. We imagine that these benefits could be conveyed more broadly to renters because they are not inherent to homeownership but, rather, to residential stability.

Before presenting our results, we detail some of the measurements and definitions we used in our analysis, especially regarding key variables such as sense of control, trust, and mental health. All data used in this analysis come from questions asked in the 2009 survey. As with all the analyses presented throughout this book, we address the challenge of selection bias introduced by respondents' self-selecting into homeownership.

Sense of control is measured using Cohen's Perceived Stress Scale (PSS), a scale that has been used in a wide variety of studies and that was designed to measure the degree to which people feel they have control over the important aspects of their lives (Cohen, Kamarck, & Mermelstein 1983). The four items in the PSS are (1) in the last month, how often have you felt that you were unable to control the important things in your life, (2) in the last month, how often have you felt confident about your ability to handle your personal problems, (3) in the last month, how often have you felt that things were going your way, and (4) in the last month, how often have you felt difficulties were piling up so high that you could not overcome them? Each of the four items in the scale has the following response options: 0 = never, 1 = almost never, 2 = sometimes, 3 = fairly often, 4 = very often.[1] Scores range from 0 (low sense of control) to 16 (high sense of control). Thus, a higher score on the scale indicates a greater sense of control.

Trust in one's neighbors was measured by the question "How much would you say you can trust your neighbors: a lot, some, only a little, or not at all?" Respondents who said they trusted their neighbors a lot were coded 1, and all others were coded 0. Thus, rather than using an abstract notion of generalized trust, we anchor perceptions of trust by asking our respondents specifically about their neighbors.

Lastly, mental health was measured using the question "During the past four weeks, have you accomplished less than you would like to as a result of any emotional problems, such as feeling depressed or anxious?"[2] Just over 14% of the sample reported that they had experienced a mental health problem in the prior month. Using these measurements to test our expectations, we now turn to the results of our analyses.

Results

In this section, we present results from several models predicting the three outcomes: sense of control, trust in neighbors, and mental health problem. In Table 4.1, we show estimates from models predicting respondents' sense of control. Results in Model 1 indicate that being a homeowner is associated with feeling a greater sense of control over one's life. With Model 2, we add household demographic variables in order to see whether the homeownership effect remains in the presence of these other factors. In both models, home-owners score about 0.6 higher on the 16-point sense of control scale, compared to similar renters.

We include in Model 2 the presence of children in the home, age, gender, education, marital status, employment, and race or ethnicity. We also include dwelling type as a potential confound of homeownership: This measure indicates whether the dwelling is a single-family house or a multifamily house, but it is not significant in any of the models. Even with the inclusion of these demographic variables, results in Model 2 show that our findings are consistent: Our analysis suggests that homeownership does, indeed, carry with it a heightened sense of control.

In addition to homeownership, the results from the mediating variables included in Model 2 illuminate two other important factors affecting a person's sense of control. First, employment status had the greatest effect of any variable: People who are unemployed, are not in the labor force, or are working part-time all have a lower sense of control than people who are working full-time. Full-time employment, at least within a lower-income population, gives people a sense of control over their lives. Second, the model also reveals that Hispanic respondents have a lower of a sense of control than other racial/ethnic groups. Next, we consider how these findings relate to trust in neighbors.

Having established a link between homeownership and perceived control, our analysis now moves to testing whether there is a similar link between homeownership and trust in one's neighbors. As described above, our expectation is that both sense of control and trust are mechanisms that link homeownership to mental health outcomes. Table 4.2 shows the results of the two models predicting trust. Both models show that homeownership is positively related to a person's trust in his or her neighbors. Model 3 indicates that homeowners are 58% more likely than similar renters to report that they feel they can trust their neighbors a lot. When the control variables are added, this homeownership effect increases somewhat.

TABLE 4.1

Sense of Control Regressed on Homeownership

	Model 1	Model 2
Homeowner	0.59*	0.60*
Children in home		−0.22
Age		−0.01
Male		0.10
Education		
Some college		−0.05
2-year degree		0.23
4-year degree		0.22
Advanced degree		0.95*
Marital status		
Divorced/separated		−0.36
Widowed		0.20
Single		−0.38
Cohabiting		−0.31
Employment		
Employed part-time		−0.84*
Retired		−0.10
Unemployed		−1.56*
Not in labor force		−1.10*
Race/ethnicity		
Black		−0.17
Hispanic		−0.74*
Other race		−0.37
Dwelling type		
Multifamily housing		−0.04
Other dwelling type		−0.29
R^2	0.01	0.08
Sample size		1,310

N = 1,310, following propensity score analysis matching renters to owners.

Estimation: Ordinary least squares regression of respondent's sense of control, measured on a scale from 0–16.

Table displays beta coefficients.

*Result is statistically significant ($p < 0.05$).

TABLE 4.2

Trust in Neighbors Regressed on Homeownership

	Model 3	Model 4
Homeowner	1.58*	1.69*
Children in home		0.89
Age		1.01
Male		0.82
Education		
Some college		1.24
2-year degree		1.50*
4-year degree		1.22
Advanced degree		1.84*
Marital status		
Divorced/separated		0.74
Widowed		1.59
Single		1.00
Cohabiting		0.91
Employment		
Employed part-time		0.79
Retired		0.93
Unemployed		0.63*
Not in labor force		1.03
Race/ethnicity		
Black		0.57*
Hispanic		0.77
Other race		0.48*
Dwelling type		
Multifamily housing		0.57*
Other dwelling type		0.92
Sample size	1,310	

N = 1,384, following propensity score analysis matching renters to owners.
Estimation: Bivariate logistic regression of whether respondent can trust their neighbors "a lot."
Table displays odds ratios.
*Result is statistically significant ($p < 0.05$).

Results from Model 4 indicate that homeowners are 69% more likely to trust their neighbors a lot.

Model 4 results also indicate statistically significant associations for several demographic variables. Trust in neighbors is higher for more educated respondents. Unemployment is associated with a lower level of trust in neighbors. The indicator for race and ethnicity shows that minorities score lower on the measure of trust in neighbors; the effect is statistically significant for blacks but not for Hispanics. The results also point to an effect for dwelling type: Compared to single-family dwellings, respondents in multifamily housing have a lower trust in neighbors.

The final step in the analysis is to determine whether either of these two mechanisms translates to a decreased likelihood of mental health problems. To assess the potential for indirect effects, we interpret findings across several models. We do control for all of the demographic variables shown in earlier models for sense of control and trust in neighbors; however, in this section we limit our presentation to the findings as they relate to a potential homeownership effect.

Table 4.3 presents results from four models predicting whether a respondent reported having experienced a mental health impairment in the four weeks preceding the interview. Model 5 shows results for homeownership, absent trust in neighbors or sense of control. Model 6 displays results for trust in neighbors while excluding homeownership and sense of control. Model 7 similarly excludes homeownership and trust in neighbors in order to assess the effect of sense of control. The final estimation, Model 8, includes all three variables. These models, presented in detail next, determine that homeownership and perceived control do decrease the risk of mental health issues, although trust in one's neighbors does not. Additionally, these models indicate that mental health impacts are not

TABLE 4.3

Mental Health Problem Regressed on Homeownership

	(5) Homeownership	(6) Trust Neighbors	(7) Sense of Control	(8) All
Homeowner	0.66*			0.80
Trust in neighbors		0.77		0.94
Sense of control			0.68*	0.68*

$N = 1,384$, following propensity score analysis matching renters to owners.

Estimation: Bivariate logistic regression of whether respondent reports experiencing a mental health problem.

Table displays odds ratios.

Model specification controls for demographics shown in prior two models (children in the home, age, gender, education, marital status, employment, race or ethnicity, and dwelling type). We omit these variables from this table to focus the presentation on testing the potential mediation of trust in neighbors and sense of control.

*Result is statistically significant ($p < 0.05$).

associated with the fact of homeownership itself but, rather, from one's sense of control.

Model 5 includes only the homeownership variable and the demographic control variables. As shown, homeowners are only 66% as likely as similar renters to have experienced a mental health problem. This means that homeowners are, indeed, less likely to experience these problems. This homeownership effect exists while controlling for demographic variables, including whether the respondent lives in single-family or multifamily housing. These estimates for dwelling type are not statistically significant in any of the models predicting mental health problems.

Model 6 tests whether people who report a great deal of trust in their neighbors are less likely to report mental health concerns. This variable is not statistically significant, indicating that the perception of trust in one's neighbors does not decrease one's risk of mental health problems.[3] While prior models documented an association between homeownership and trust, this model indicates that trust in neighbors is unrelated to mental health.

Model 7 tests whether there is a relationship between sense of control and mental health. The model does reveal a relationship: It shows that a one-point increase in the 16-point sense of control scale is associated with a 32% decline in the risk of mental health impairment. Thus, people who feel more in control of the important aspects of their lives are less likely to report mental health problems.[4]

Lastly, Model 8 combines all three predictors: homeownership, trust in neighbors, and sense of control. By combining results from Models 5, 7, and 8, we can interpret whether sense of control mediates the homeownership effect. Model 8 shows that people with a greater sense of control over their lives are less likely to have mental health difficulties. Note that homeownership is not statistically significant in Model 8. Given this change (compared to Model 5), the result suggests that sense of control mediates homeownership. Once Model 8 accounts for the sense of control stemming from homeownership, there is no independent relationship between homeownership and mental health.

Together these model results identify the following four relationships: (1) homeownership predicts a person's sense of control, (2) homeownership predicts mental health when sense of control is excluded, (3) sense of control predicts mental health, and (4) the effect of homeownership on mental health is reduced when sense of control is included in the model. Additional testing of mediation (not displayed in the table) indicates that sense of control mediated approximately 72% of the effect of homeownership on mental health, meaning that one's sense of control is the primary conveyer of mental health benefits.[5]

Thus, our analysis reveals that homeownership is linked with mental health through the mediating factor of sense of control. Interestingly, while the analysis reveals that homeowners are more likely than renters to feel they can trust their neighbors, this greater sense of trust does not translate into a reduced risk of mental health problems. Finally, the heightened sense of control that comes from homeownership entirely explains the decrease in the likelihood of experiencing a mental health problem.

Conclusion

Our analysis supports some, though not all, of our initial expectations. Homeowners do report a greater sense of control over their lives than renters, they are more likely to feel that they can trust their neighbors than renters, and people who feel a greater sense of control over their lives are less likely to experience mental health difficulties. However, contrary to expectations, people who feel that they can trust their neighbors are not found to be less likely to experience mental health difficulties. Further analysis indicated that that sense of control is the primary mechanism by which this mental health benefit is transferred, rather than homeownership itself. From these results, we draw two important conclusions: one for social disorganization theory broadly and the other for the study of homeownership.

First, our findings suggest that social disorganization theory would benefit from an expansion that could accommodate harder-to-measure, subjective indicators of neighborhood conditions, including trust and a person's sense of control. Social bonds and trust in one's neighbors have traditionally been measured at the community level and have been taken as objective features of a community. However, we find that people may perceive neighborhood conditions differently based on their homeownership status within the neighborhood and based on individual differences such as race and ethnicity, marriage, and employment. Additionally, whether by virtue of their financial interest in the neighborhood or their sense of ownership in the community, homeowners as a group are more likely than renters to feel a sense of trust in their neighbors.

Lastly, our analysis also advances research on homeownership not only by demonstrating that homeownership is associated with a reduced risk of mental health difficulties, but also by assessing *why* it has this impact. This study demonstrates that homeownership is associated with a reduced risk of mental health problems because it provides people with a meaningful sense of control over their lives. The analysis takes a step toward developing a more comprehensive theory of homeownership by specifying the mechanism that connects homeownership with the important outcome of mental health. The mechanism that we identified, sense of control, can likely be conveyed to other households through pathways other than homeownership itself; therefore, this research can contributes to policy discussions about how to improve the lives of renters. We will build upon this preliminary effort in Chapter 9, where we test several mechanisms simultaneously, across health and civic engagement outcomes, in order to understand how and why homeownership conveys the benefits that have been associated with it.

Notes

1. The scale contains four items, two of which are reverse-coded.

2. This question was adopted from the mental health component of the SF-12, a reliable health status scale that measures physical and mental health (Jenkinson et al. 1997). This question has been used in other studies as a reliable single-item indicator of mental health (Elo, Leppänen, & Jahkola 2003; Zhang 2007) and yields similar results as the full SF-12 scale (Diehr, Chen, Patrick, Feng, & Yasui 2005). In our analysis, CAP respondents who answered yes were coded 1, all others 0.

3. In fact, adding the trust-in-neighbors measure does not substantially change any of the coefficients in the model.

4. And, of course, the direction of causation could be the other way: People with better mental health feel more in control of their lives.

5. This test satisfies the criteria for mediation, and the Sobel-Goodman mediation test, which indicates whether the intervening variable being tested transmits effects from an independent variable to a dependent variable. These results indicate how much of the impact that the independent variable has on the outcome is being carried through the mediator.

5 Local Voting

IN PREVIOUS CHAPTERS, we discussed how homeownership seems to help homeowners experience better physical and mental health outcomes than similar renters. These health outcomes have a direct impact on a person's quality of life. Similarly, a person's quality of life can be affected by his or her relationships with others and by conditions in his or her community. Beginning with this chapter, we turn from individual health to engagement with the broader community. Our focus in this chapter is on one particular form of civic engagement—voting in local elections. Political engagement through voting is a crucial element of democracy and is one of the most accessible avenues through which ordinary citizens can participate in civic life. Thus, research that suggests ways to increase the level of participation in elections can contribute to a more representative democracy.

In this chapter, we evaluate whether homeowners are more likely to vote in local elections than renters and, if so, whether this pattern is realized equally for homeowners across neighborhoods or whether it is context-dependent (Engelhardt, Eriksen, Gale, & Mills 2010; Kingston, Thompson, & Eichar 1984). More specifically, we test whether homeowners in more advantaged neighborhoods are more likely to vote than homeowners in disadvantaged neighborhoods.

This analysis offers two key contributions to the study of the social impacts of homeownership, particularly with regards to voting. First, it addresses the role of homeownership in motivating local voting participation among lower-income citizens. Second, our findings inform the broader debate about the value of encouraging homeownership in disadvantaged areas.

While policymakers have long focused on promoting homeownership among lower-income families as a means of wealth building, some scholars have questioned this position (McCabe 2016; Rohe et al. 2002). These scholars argue that neighborhood revitalization efforts aimed at increasing homeownership in disadvantaged neighborhoods can result in homeowners' feeling trapped in depreciating neighborhoods that offer them few opportunities for civic or community involvement. Our research offers empirical evidence as to whether neighborhood disadvantage alters the degree to which homeowners participate in local political activities.

Background

A key element of a democratic society is the vote. If a government is to be by and for the people, as the United States aspires to be, then citizens must participate in elections in order to have a say in local and national decisions. However, voter turnout in the United States is notoriously low, with only 25.8% turnout in mayoral elections on average (Holbrook & Weinschenk 2014). Thus, it is important to pay attention to which factors influence citizens to exercise their right to vote in order to bolster voter turnout and ensure true representation. In this chapter, we test, first, whether homeownership influences this behavior and, second, whether the relative advantage or disadvantage of a particular neighborhood affects the homeowners' likelihood of voting.

> We love our house and don't plan on moving.

Researchers have identified three key reasons to believe that homeowners are, indeed, more likely to participate in local rather than national elections: their financial interest in their neighborhood, their hampered mobility compared to renters, and perhaps even their attachment to their neighborhoods by virtue of their residential stability. First, homeowners have a financial motive to maintain desirable neighborhood and property conditions, and local political participation not only yields quality-of-life benefits but can also result in long-term economic benefits for homeowners (Fischel 2001). On the contrary, renters experience the same quality-of-life benefits from political participation but not the economic ones; in fact, local improvements might actually translate into increased costs for renters as rents rise in response to a neighborhood's increasing desirability (DiPasquale & Glaeser 1999).

> I bought this home thinking I would live here until I found something that I liked better, but the cost of homes was going up so much that I couldn't afford to move . . . so I am stuck here.

Second, homeowners have substantially less flexibility to move when they are unhappy with neighborhood conditions. In contrast, renters can more easily relocate if community conditions worsen. Orbell and Uno (1972) described how people make choices about responding to unfavorable neighborhood conditions, and argued that people have three options: leave the neighborhood, attempt to change the neighborhood, or do nothing. Setting aside the "do nothing" option, this amounts to an "exit or voice" decision (Hirschman 1970). Homeowners living in declining neighborhoods often confront substantial barriers to relocation. They may face difficulty selling their homes and may even have to accept a loss if house prices have fallen. Thus, they may be motivated to try to improve or maintain their neighborhoods through political and civic participation, not only as a wealth-building activity but as a lower-cost alternative to moving (Cox 1982). Renters, however, incur fewer expenses when they move; for renters, the benefits of moving may outweigh the costs.

> I really enjoy where I live. It is a safe place to grow up...I have great neighbors.

Finally, homeowners may be more active in local politics than renters because they have a greater attachment to their communities simply by virtue of being homeowners. As we have discussed in previous chapters, homeowners tend to be more satisfied with their communities in general (Rossi & Weber 1996), and this may translate to a greater inclination to participate in local elections. We could expect homeowners to be more politically involved in their communities because they feel more connected to their neighborhoods because they own a physical piece of it.

Prior empirical research has also illuminated several aspects of homeowners' political participation, including voting. While general political involvement and voting were found to be unrelated to homeownership in a field experiment by Engelhardt and colleagues (2010), other studies have found that homeowners are more likely than renters to participate in voluntary associations, local political groups, and nonprofessional organizations (Cox 1982; DiPasquale & Glaeser 1999; Guest & Oropesa 1986; Rossi & Weber 1996). Rossi and Weber (1996) analyzed a variety of nationally representative datasets and found that owners were in general more engaged in local politics than renters and were more likely to vote in national elections. Herbert and Belsky (2008) reviewed the research on voting behaviors and found that a majority of studies conclude that homeowners are more likely to vote than renters.

However, this body of research cannot be taken as conclusive evidence that homeownership itself drives voting because, like much of the previous research on the social benefits of homeownership, most of these studies have failed to address the issues of selection bias. Exceptions include the work of DiPasquale and Glaeser (1999) and Engelhardt and colleagues (2010). Rohe and colleagues (2000) also highlight the selectivity concern in suggesting that the relationship between ownership and political participation may be spurious because the possibility that people who are politically active are more likely to *become* homeowners in the first place cannot be ruled out. Prior research has also overlooked the possibility that the relationship between homeownership and local voting may be moderated by other factors. Gilderbloom and Markham (1995) compared the political participation of owners and renters by income and found that wealthier owners were more politically active than wealthier renters. However, there was no difference between owners and renters with incomes below their communities' medians.

Income may be a part of the tangle of causality connecting homeownership with voting outcomes. Some researchers believe that low-income residents are less politically active or engaged in civic life than other groups due to the relative lack of opportunities for activism in disadvantaged areas (Wilson 1990). Lower-income neighborhoods may have fewer organizations and associations focused on local issues, and residents may have less time to devote to community activities. If true, this relative lack of political engagement means that some of the most disadvantaged citizens may be cut off from the local political structures that could lead to increased opportunities. More recent research has indicated that economic disadvantage can actually spur political activity when people have a sense that positive change is possible or when they have experienced positive past interactions with government (Lawless & Fox 2001).

Another variable of interest is neighborhood disadvantage, which researchers have studied at length. Researchers have suggested that people who live in neighborhoods with higher crime rates or more public disorder experience lower levels of hope regarding the potential for change, civic engagement, and neighborhood satisfaction (Sampson & Raudenbush 1999). If residents feel they lack access to social and cultural resources, they may view political participation as futile and resign themselves to living in an undesirable area (Brady, Verba, & Schlozman 1995). On the other hand, homeowners in disadvantaged areas could

> I would like to move because I don't feel safe—this neighborhood is rough.

> The neighborhood wasn't good when I moved in, but it has gotten much better over the years. The riff-raff is gone...it has become a positive experience.

actually become more politically active in certain circumstances. Additionally, low-income families are more dependent on social ties for support than wealthier families, and they derive greater well-being from their community-based support networks (Gladow & Ray 1986). Therefore, even if neighborhood conditions decline, relocating may not be a viable or even a desirable option for lower-income homeowners. Indeed, one study found that lower-income families are less likely than middle-class families to translate neighborhood dissatisfaction into a move (South & Deane 1993). Taken together, these findings suggest that neighborhood context is an important consideration when examining the association between homeownership and local political participation.

In this analysis, we focus on the relationship between homeownership and voting. Building on existing research, we address selection bias by including in our first-stage model those factors that have been associated with homeownership, such as household income, education, and race or ethnicity. Then, after adjusting for this selectivity, we analyze how the neighborhood context may interact with homeownership to alter the likelihood that lower-income respondents vote in local elections.

Analysis

Based on the body of research outlined above, we developed two key research questions: (1) whether homeownership is associated with a higher likelihood of local voting participation and (2) whether neighborhood disadvantage is a moderating factor that alters the likelihood that a person will vote locally, over and above the impact of homeownership itself. We base this analysis on the following conceptual model, which illustrates our view of the complex relationship among homeownership, voting in local elections, and neighborhood conditions (Fig. 5.1).

To examine our ideas about homeownership, voting, and neighborhood context, we review certain elements of our survey data before describing the measurements regarding key concepts like voting participation and neighborhood disadvantage.

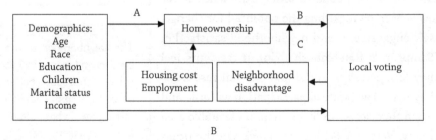

FIGURE 5.1 Conceptual diagram of the relationship between homeownership, demographics, and local voting.

To measure local voting participation, we relied on survey responses. Participants were asked a series of survey questions, including "Are you registered to vote where you live now?" And, if so, "Did you vote in the last local election?" There is likely some overreporting of voting, since estimates based on National Election Survey data indicate that between 25% and 30% of respondents misreport whether they voted in the prior election; the vast majority of these are people who report having voted when they did not (Tanur 1992). In our study, the homeownership effect will not be biased as long as homeowners and renters are equally likely to overreport voting. However, we do not know whether the tendency of people to overreport their voting behavior would be more common among homeowners, which could bias the homeownership effect that we investigate here.

Second, we measure neighborhood disadvantage at the census-tract level using an index based on research by Sampson and colleagues (2002). These researchers use the percentage of single parents, black residents, unemployed persons, families on public assistance, and households below the poverty line to represent the latent concept of localized community wealth and economic advantage, particularly the geographic isolation and multiple layers of disadvantage experienced in some poor, predominantly nonwhite, urban areas.[1] Some indicators, such as "percent black" and "percent female-headed households," used in Sampson's index are used here due to their prominence in work on concentrated disadvantage. While these factors themselves do not *cause* neighborhood disadvantage, they are *associated* and *confounded* with concentrated disadvantage in a contemporary U.S. context due to a variety of historical, social, and structural factors. As Sampson (2009) writes on the subject of race and poverty, "race and the multiple dimensions of disadvantage are ecologically intertwined and thus confounded at the neighborhood level in most large U.S. cities" (p. 265). Using these definitions and research questions, we present the results of our analysis.

Results

As in our other analyses, we first establish whether homeownership is associated with the outcome, here local voting (testing links A and B in our conceptual model, or Fig. 5.1). We use one model to adjust for the selectivity of demographic factors on the decision to own or rent (Link A) and a second to test the association between homeownership and local voting participation (Link B).[2] Descriptive statistics for key variables are presented in Table 5.1.

Table 5.2 presents the second half of our analysis, which examines whether neighborhood disadvantage and homeownership, in addition to other household demographic factors, predict local voting behavior. We run three different

TABLE 5.1

Local Voting—Descriptive Statistics

Variable	Renters		Owners	
	Mean	SD	Mean	SD
Relative income	.45	0.29	0.67	0.31
Months in neighborhood	34.42	56.73	38.39	66.86
Neighborhood disadvantage	.36	0.66	0.13	0.83
Relative homeownership cost	2.10	0.14	2.10	0.22

N = 1,836. SD = standard deviation.
"Relative homeownership cost" is a ratio of the median monthly housing cost for owners holding a mortgage to the median rent paid by renters; it is calculated at the metropolitan statistical area level using census data.

models. Model 1 tests our first research question: Is homeownership associated with a higher likelihood of voter participation in local elections? Model 2 tests another research question: Is neighborhood context a significant factor in determining voter participation, regardless of whether a person is a homeowner? Our final model puts these two research questions together to test whether a person's neighborhood context *and* status as a homeowner or a renter is associated with a higher likelihood of voter participation.

Our first model shows that homeowners are, in fact, more likely than renters to have voted in the most recent local election. This model also shows that certain key demographic factors are statistically significant: race, age, marriage, education, and the presence of children. Hispanic and "other race" respondents who were registered to vote are much less likely to have voted compared to whites. Older respondents are slightly more likely to have voted, and so are single respondents. Respondents at all other education levels are significantly more likely to vote compared to those who have only a high school degree or less. The presence of children in the home is associated with a decline in voting likelihood. Relative income and length of time in the neighborhood, interestingly, have no effect on local voting participation.

Model 2 tests whether neighborhood disadvantage is associated with the likelihood of a person voting in a local election and reveals a small yet significant relationship. People who live in more disadvantaged neighborhoods are slightly *more* likely to have voted in their most recent local election. Our final test, seen in Model 3, reveals that neighborhood disadvantage does, indeed, moderate the relationship between homeownership and local voting: Homeowners in disadvantaged neighborhoods are even more likely to vote in local elections than either owners in less disadvantaged areas or renters in comparable neighborhoods. Thus the lower-income households reporting the greatest likelihood

TABLE 5.2

Local Voting Regressed on Homeownership and Neighborhood Disadvantage

	Model 1	Model 2	Model 3
Homeowner (vs. renter)	1.38*	1.44*	1.37*
Neighborhood disadvantage		0.17*	0.01
Homeownership disadvantage			0.22*
Black (vs. white)	0.09	−0.01	−0.02
Hispanic	−1.66*	−1.80*	−1.84*
Other race	−1.41*	−1.40*	−1.51*
Age	0.03*	0.03*	0.03*
Single (vs. married)	0.41*	0.40*	0.37*
Divorced	−0.08	−0.04	−0.07
Some college (vs. high school diploma or less)	1.44*	1.45*	1.45*
College degree	1.78*	1.72*	1.68*
Advanced degree	1.52*	1.43*	1.38*
Child(ren) in home	−0.38*	−0.35*	−0.38*
Relative income	−0.30*	−0.31*	−0.31*
Months in neighborhood	0.00	0.00	0.00

$N = 1,836$.

Estimation: Bivariate logistic regression of whether respondent reports voting in the last local election.

Table displays coefficients from a bivariate probit model. Homeownership has been instrumented (using relative homeownership cost for the metropolitan statistical area and employment status).

*Result is statistically significant ($p < 0.05$).

of voting in local elections are those people who own homes in disadvantaged neighborhoods.

Figure 5.2 presents a graph of this interaction between homeownership and neighborhood disadvantage. The figure shows the predicted probability of a respondent having voted in the most recent local election based on Model 3. As is shown, there is a substantial gap between owners and renters, with homeowners predicted to vote at much higher levels than renters.[3] Figure 5.2 shows that as neighborhood disadvantage increases, homeowners' likelihood of voting also increases. From the least to the most disadvantaged neighborhood, homeowners' predicted probability of voting increases by around 30%. Voting by renters, however, remains nearly constant in different types of neighborhoods and is lower than voting by owners.

In short, as neighborhood disadvantage increases, homeowners are more likely to be politically active at the local level, where their actions have the most potential

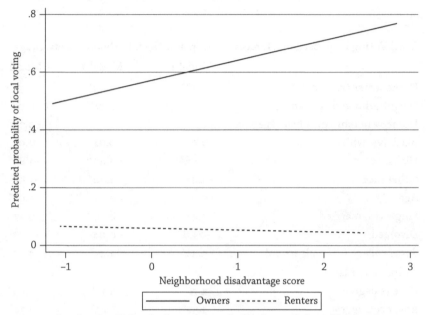

FIGURE 5.2 Local voting higher for homeowners in disadvantaged neighborhoods.

to improve their neighborhoods and communities. This result implies that home-ownership can be a catalyst for voting, a very important type of goal-seeking civic engagement.

Conclusion

The objective of this chapter was twofold: to test the relationship between home-ownership and voting, and to test whether neighborhood disadvantage moder-ates that relationship. Concerning the relationship between homeownership and voting, we found that homeownership does have an independent effect on local political participation: Owners are more likely than renters to have voted in their most recent local elections. This finding confirms results from previous stud-ies on political participation and homeownership and suggests that, contrary to Rohe and colleagues' (2000) suggestion, the relationship is not spurious—that is, the homeowner effect is not explained entirely by selectivity into owning, nor by neighborhood conditions. Concerning neighborhood disadvantage, we also uncovered an independent effect on political participation: People in disadvan-taged neighborhoods are more likely to have voted in their most recent local elec-tion regardless of their homeownership status.

Finally, our analysis revealed that—in our dataset of lower-income households—homeowners who live in disadvantaged neighborhoods are more likely to vote in local elections than both renters living in similar neighborhoods *and* homeowners in more advantaged areas. Thus, as neighborhood distress increases, homeowners are more likely to vote locally, while renters' local voting behavior remains relatively constant. Taken together, our findings support the idea that homeownership among lower-income households can spur political participation at the local level. Further, we discovered that homeownership may act as a catalyst for political participation in disadvantaged neighborhoods.

Our analysis suggests that homeownership can provide a pathway to positive social change in two ways. First, by increasing political involvement within disadvantaged neighborhoods, homeownership contributes to the empowerment of these communities through local voting. Second, homeownership can also benefit communities as a whole because involved, engaged citizens are more likely to actualize the positive changes they seek for their communities. These positive outcomes suggest that low-income homeownership is a positive social force.

At the same time, individual-level costs associated with homeownership in disadvantaged neighborhoods must be acknowledged. While homeownership brings collective benefit to disadvantaged areas, individual owners who live in these communities may invest a disproportionate amount of time and resources in creating improvements relative to owners in more desirable areas (Galster 1987). Any policies intended to promote homeownership in disadvantaged areas must consider whether potential homeowners would be better off purchasing elsewhere.

Whether homeowners stay in disadvantaged areas out of necessity or by choice, they do demonstrate a commitment to improving their neighborhoods through local political involvement. Our research shows that lower-income owners capitalize on the local voting opportunities they see. This benefits individual homeowners by protecting their wealth and long-term equity, and also benefits struggling neighborhoods by promoting active citizenship and fostering a sense of shared community and civic engagement that can translate into positive change.

Notes

1. Each element of the index is transformed to a z-score, and they are summed together and divided by five (Benson, Fox, DeMaris, & Van Wyk 2003).

2. Owners are coded 1 and renters are coded 0. This measure is then instrumented and becomes the key independent variable in the second equation predicting voting.

3. These lines show the predicted probability of voting, not whether any given respondent actually voted.

6 Civic Engagement

ONE LONGSTANDING JUSTIFICATION for homeownership is its assumed increase of owners' "civic engagement"—that is, citizen participation in the local community. Civic engagement requires time and resources, but it can provide important benefits to individuals and their communities. As McBride, Sherraden, and Pritzker (2006) explain, "Civic engagement . . . is considered [to be] a means for developing skills and capacity, increasing tolerance among peoples, building community, supporting collective action on common goals, and girding democratic governance through [the] representation of interests."

In the nineteenth century, French political theorist Alexis de Tocqueville noted in his famous *Democracy in America* that, in the United States, Americans were joining together in associations (Tocqueville 1862). Today, many researchers, such as Robert Putnam (the author of the 2001 book *Bowling Alone*) and Theda Skocpol (1997), argue that associations among friends and neighbors have declined significantly over time, but they tend to disagree about the causes of this decline. Some say that technology has replaced face-to-face social engagement, and others say that Americans, perhaps rightly given the influence of money in politics, "no longer feel that they can effectively band together to get things done" through civic engagement (Skocpol 1997). Nevertheless, there is consensus that civic engagement is a positive force. To this effect, research has found that communities with high levels of civic engagement are more cohesive and have fewer social problems and lower crime rates (McBride et al. 2006).

Researchers disagree about whether homeownership is connected to civic engagement. While some researchers believe that homeownership gives people a deep stake in the future of their neighborhood, others believe that homeowners may actually withdraw from public life. Research has linked homeownership to a variety of positive social outcomes such as increased community involvement, more diverse social capital networks, and greater political participation (Dietz & Haurin 2003; DiPasquale & Glaeser 1999; Haurin, Parcel, & Haurin 2002). Putnam (2000) specifically points to a rise in single-family homeownership as a key contributor to the decline of civic engagement in America.

In this chapter, we ask whether low- and moderate-income homeowners are more likely than similar renters to be civically engaged. Research supports the idea that homeowners are more likely to be involved in their communities, but whether this link is due to homeownership itself or other factors associated with homeownership is less clear (Herbert & Belsky 2008). In the prior chapter, we partly addressed this concern about causality by first modeling the decision to own or rent. We found that one form of civic engagement—voting in local elections—is more likely among lower-income homeowners, especially homeowners who live in disadvantaged neighborhoods. The reasons for this relationship are not yet clear; it is conceivable that homeowners in less-desirable neighborhoods become more engaged with their communities in order to do something about their circumstances, given that they lack the mobility of comparable renters. Furthermore, even homeowners who do feel they have the option to move may be reluctant to do so, instead becoming more civically engaged because they feel a stronger sense of attachment to their local communities than renters do.

However, scholars have cautioned that neighborhood revitalization efforts that focus on increasing homeownership in disadvantaged neighborhoods could result in homeowners feeling trapped in depreciating neighborhoods that offer few opportunities for civic or community involvement (Rohe et al. 2002). In fact, neighborhood disadvantage has been linked to other negative outcomes such as lower levels of trust, lack of citizen participation in community groups, and decreased involvement in community life (Furstenburg 1993; Skogan 1990; Wilson 1996; Wilson & Kelling 1982). This raises an interesting and important question about the promotion of homeownership in disadvantaged neighborhoods: Does increasing homeownership in these areas promote civic participation, or does it lock lower-income families into disadvantaged areas where they are likely to withdraw from community life?

Background

Lower-income citizens have historically had lower levels of civic engagement than the general population. The result is that low- and moderate-income households do not fully voice their interests in the democratic process (Verba, Schlozman, & Brady 1995). Because civic engagement is a precursor to community influence, the relative lack of engagement among lower-income populations is likely to translate into less political and social influence. Therefore, it is important to understand which factors might increase civic engagement among historically marginalized populations in order to work toward higher levels of representation and influence. Identifying ways to increase civic engagement by lower-income people can increase participatory democracy and can thereby empower citizens.

In this chapter, our primary research question concerns whether and how changes in homeownership status and mobility influence civic engagement. This analysis offers two important contributions to the field, one theoretical and one methodological. First, our work focuses on lower-income homeowners. Most research to date on civic engagement has found that lower-income people are less engaged in civil society (Uslaner & Brown 2005), and understanding what factors could increase their involvement is important (McBride et al. 2006). Second, as with all of the analysis in this book, we empirically consider the potential for respondent selectivity to bias the homeownership effect, in order to address this key shortcoming of many earlier studies on the social impacts of homeownership (Dietz & Haurin 2003). Before we begin our analysis, we define the concept of civic engagement and its relationship to homeownership.

As used in this chapter, the term "civic engagement" refers to citizen participation in civic *organizations* and *processes*. For example, membership in the Rotary Club or the Girl Scouts is an example of participation in civic organizations, while voting or attending a school board meeting is an example of participation in civic processes. The key aspect of civic engagement is that it represents engagement between the individual and a larger group, organization, or social process.

Researchers have identified two distinct forms of civic engagement: *expressive* engagement and *instrumental* engagement (Son & Lin 2008; Swaroop & Morenoff 2006). Expressive civic engagement consists of actions motivated by a sense of identity as a member of a community and is not motivated by an explicit goal. Examples of expressive civic engagement include having frequent conversations with neighbors or organizing community social events. Instrumental civic engagement, on the other hand, consists of goal-oriented actions that address the functional and pragmatic concerns of residents in a community. Joining a neighborhood organization, voting, and participating in local politics are examples of instrumental civic engagement. The key distinction between the two types of civic engagement is the intent: Activities primarily motivated by community identity are expressive, while those motivated by problem solving are instrumental. These forms of civic engagement are analogous to what other scholars label "social" and "political" engagement (Putnam 2000).

Civic engagement, both expressive and instrumental, produces tangible benefits within a community and also contributes to the formation of the trust and shared norms that foster the development of social capital (Putnam 2000). Over the past few decades, much of the discussion of civic engagement has focused on whether or not it is declining in Western society (Ladd 1996; Perrin 2006; Putnam 1995). While this debate certainly has merit, it remains important to clarify our understanding of what factors lead to higher levels of civic engagement. To address this challenge, in this chapter we examine the relationship between homeownership and the two types of civic engagement by measuring whether people converse often with their neighbors (which represents expressive engagement) and whether they participate in an organized neighborhood group (which represents instrumental engagement).

Research on the link between homeownership and civic engagement among lower-income populations has produced mixed results, and many earlier studies have been critiqued for methodological flaws, limited data, and imprecise measures (Herbert & Belsky 2008). Rohe and Stegman (1994b) found that homeowners were more likely to join neighborhood-based groups but not other types of community organizations. A pair of studies by Pratt (1986; 1987) found that homeowners were more active in several types of community groups, but these studies failed to account for selection bias. Based on their review of the research on the relationship between homeownership and civic engagement, Dietz and Haurin (2003, p. 430) concluded that "Given the mixed empirical results and the questionable methodology of many studies where sorting, endogeneity, and unobserved variables are not accounted for, no strong conclusions can be drawn at this time." Thus, it is still unclear whether homeownership influences civic engagement.

While a link between homeownership and civic engagement has not been conclusively established, three mechanisms can potentially explain why they may be related. Within economics, scholars have tended to focus on financial explanations and presume that homeowners have a financial reason to be more engaged in their communities (Dietz & Haurin 2003). Other researchers focus on a broader "collection of interests," which combine to determine a person's engagement choices

(Davis 1991; Saunders 1978). Finally, returning to Putnam's (1995; 2000) view, it is also possible that homeownership might be associated with declines in instrumental civic engagement due to decreased mobility, meaning that homeowners feel more satisfied with their neighborhoods and believe that there is less need for community activism. We consider each of these explanations here.

Much of the early research on homeownership and civic engagement focused on the financial motivations that may prompt homeowners to become involved in local civic organizations. Unlike renters, homeowners have a financial stake in maintaining desirable neighborhood conditions since the value of their homes is partially tied to the larger community (Rohe & Stewart 1996). For this reason, civic participation yields not only quality-of-life benefits but also long-term economic benefits to homeowners. Renters, conversely, experience the same quality-of-life and intrinsic benefits associated with civic participation, but not the economic ones. In fact, research suggests that renters may actually experience negative economic consequences of civic participation because rents are likely to increase in neighborhoods with active civic organizations (DiPasquale & Glaeser 1999).

If this explanation is supported empirically, linking homeownership with civic engagement via simple financial self-interest, we would expect to find that homeowners are more active in instrumental, or goal-seeking, activities, but we would not necessarily expect to find higher rates of expressive engagement, since only instrumental civic activities should raise property values. This means that while financial motives may explain why a homeowner would lobby to have a local park built, they fail to account for forms of expressive engagement such as building relationships with neighbors.

The second explanation moves beyond a strictly financial explanation for why homeowners may be more involved in civic life. In *Contested Ground* (1991), John Emmeus Davis describes domestic property as a "bundle of interests," implying that acquiring a given property also means acquiring the bundle of interests associated with it. This idea is based on an understanding of "interests" that includes more than financial interests alone. Two types of interests that are particularly relevant when examining homeownership and civic engagement are *use* interests and *exchange* interests.

> What I like most is that the neighbors are far away and nobody bothers us. I also like that the grocery stores are near and the hospital is near.
>
> —Homeowner

A use interest is based on expected usage, such as an interest in forming social ties with neighbors because doing so provides friendship, or an interest in building a neighborhood playground because it will give children a place to play. Both renters and owners have use interests that motivate civic engagement. However, owners may have more use interests than renters if they expect to remain in the same dwelling longer. Returning to the example of the local park, a renter may expect to move out of the neighborhood after a short period of time, so efforts spent to build or maintain a park would bring only temporary returns. An owner, however, may have more of an interest in putting forth an effort since he or she expects to use the park for many years. This is not a simply financial motivation but, rather, is based on harder-to-measure concepts of use value.

On the other hand, exchange interests, according to Davis, vary between renters and homeowners. An exchange interest is rooted in the exchange value (market value) of the property. This is akin to the first explanation of civic engagement described above and is characterized by financial self-interest. Because

> It's nothing to be excited about...it's just a place to live.
> —Renter

renters do not own their dwellings and therefore cannot sell them, they lack exchange interests. This theoretically translates into the potential for a meaningful difference in behaviors, whereby renters are less likely to engage in civic activities that are aimed solely at increasing the exchange values in a neighborhood.

According to this theory, when someone buys or rents a home, he or she does more than simply become the occupant of a physical structure. The person also becomes the occupant of a unique package of property interests, both economic and not, characterized by whether one is a homeowner or a renter, neighborhood characteristics, and expected mobility. This combination of use and exchange interests influences behavior. If we were to find empirical evidence to support this view, then we would see that homeowners express higher levels of both expressive and instrumental civic engagement.

The third explanation about the connection between homeownership and civic engagement hinges on the idea of residential stability. This argument rests on the assumption that a person who remains in place for a relatively long period of time is satisfied with that place. One study found that the median length of stay in a residence was two years for renters

> Homeownership gives me a lot of independence. My neighbors are friendly...no intruders, no crime.

and eight years for homeowners (Rohe et al. 2002). Prior research has found that, when controlling for actual neighborhood conditions, long-term residents are more likely to report feeling satisfied with their neighborhoods (Rohe & Stegman 1994a). Even within low-income, disadvantaged neighborhoods, homeowners are more likely than renters to recommend their neighborhood as a good place to live (Yeo, Grinstein-Weiss, & Taylor 2010). It is possible that the decreased mobility, or residential stability, leads homeowners to hold more favorable views of their communities and, in turn, to perceive fewer problems to confront. Residents may be willing to get involved, but simply perceive no need to do so because they don't think there are community concerns that need to be resolved.

There has been some research to support this contention. According to Oliver (1999), local political participation is lower in affluent areas than in middle-income areas because there are fewer perceived problems and therefore less need to be engaged. Oliver concluded that "contentment with local politics breeds apathy toward local affairs and lower participation" (1999, p. 204). Similarly, Kim and Ball-Rokeach (2006) found that the longer people remained in their residence, the more likely they were to report a feeling of neighborhood belonging. However, they were not more likely to actually participate in neighborhood organizations.

If our analysis provides empirical evidence to support this view, we will find that homeowners have lower rates of instrumental, or goal-seeking, civic engagement. However, homeowners may have higher rates of expressive civic engagement because of their relative stability. Because they remain in their neighborhoods for longer than renters do, they may have more time to form social ties with their neighbors and may feel attached to their neighborhoods (Rohe et al. 2002). Taylor found that "in more stable neighborhoods, residents feel closer to the community and to one another" (1996, p. 63). Kasarda and Janowitz (1974) also found that length of residence was the key factor predicting the strength and number of social ties people had with their neighbors, and that these social ties helped to strengthen residents' sense of attachment to their neighborhoods. In summary, homeowners' decreased residential mobility may lead them to feel closer to their neighbors, prompting more expressive engagement.

Our analysis seeks to understand whether or not homeownership encourages households to become civically engaged, either instrumentally or expressively. As in several other chapters, we also consider the possibility that outcomes are related to residential stability rather than homeownership itself. The three theories, one primarily financial, one based on a collection of different interests, and one based on residential stability, inform the following analysis.

Analysis

Based on the discussion outlined above, we present three possible outcomes, which are illustrated in Table 6.1. First, if the relationship between homeownership and civic engagement is explained by financial self-interest, we would expect homeowners to have higher levels of instrumental engagement than renters do, but we would *not* expect to see differences in expressive engagement between homeowners and renters. This is because if the financial interests explanation holds,

TABLE 6.1

Expected Relationships Between Homeownership and Civic
Engagement

Theoretical Perspective	Type of Civic Engagement	
	Instrumental	Expressive
Financial self-interest	+	(no effect)
Collection of interests	+	+
Residential stability	−	+

homeowners will be motivated by goal-oriented, utilitarian actions that protect their neighborhood interests.

The second possibility concerns the "collection of interests" explanation, which combines the ideas of financial interests, use interests, and exchange interests. If the relationship between homeowner-ship and civic engagement is explained by a collection of interests, then we would expect homeowners to have higher levels of *both* instrumental engagement *and* expressive engagement. This is because, in the "collection of interests" explanation, a wide variety of factors combine to determine a person's civic engagement activities. However, we would also expect mobility to play a role in predicting civic engagement, since the length of time someone expects to live in an area would directly affect the use value of getting involved in the neighborhood. Therefore, under this "collection of interests" explanation, both homeowners and renters who plan to move would have lower levels of civic engagement than people who do not plan to move.

> I am very friendly with everyone in my neighborhood.
> —Homeowner

Finally, there is the explanation that homeownership affects civic engagement via decreased residential mobility. This explanation predicts that homeowners will have lower levels of instrumental engagement because they see fewer neighborhood problems to confront. However, they will have higher levels of expressive engagement than renters because their decreased mobility may allow them to form stronger social ties with their neighbors.

We test these explanations using several approaches. First, we determine whether there is an association between homeownership and both types of civic engagement. Second, we use propensity score models to evaluate how well the initial models account for selection bias.[1] Third, we test whether homeowners were more engaged *before* they became homeowners and whether they became more engaged *after* purchasing a home. Finally, we test whether residential mobility has a different impact on civic engagement for renters than for homeowners.

TABLE 6.2

Civic Engagement, Homeownership Status, and Mobility—Descriptive
Statistics Across Time Points

Variable	2004	2007
Civic Engagement		
Neighborhood group member (instrumental)	17%	19%
Talk frequently with neighbors (expressive)	40%	36%
Homeownership Status and Mobility		
Homeowner	62%	64%
Owner who moved (between 2004 and 2007)		44%
Renter who did not move		14%
Renter who became homeowner		7%
Owner who became renter		4%
Owner who moved		13%
Renter who moved		18%

Sample size is 2,215. Summed percentages are inexact due to rounding.

Descriptive statistics for key variables are presented in Table 6.2. Before presenting the results of our analysis, we explain how we measure the two outcomes,
instrumental and expressive civic engagement.

There are two key outcomes for this analysis: instrumental civic engagement
and expressive civic engagement. We measure instrumental civic engagement as
participation in any neighborhood group or organization.[2] In 2004, 17% of respondents were members of some kind of neighborhood group. As shown in Table 6.2,
this figure rose to 19% by 2007.

The second key outcome is expressive civic engagement. We analyze this outcome as a binary indicator of whether or not a respondent reported having frequent conversations with his or her neighbors.[3] Table 6.2 shows that, in 2004, 40%
of respondents reported having frequent conversations with neighbors. However,
in 2007, this figure dropped to 36%.

The key independent variables of interest in this study are homeownership status and mobility. Table 6.2 shows that in 2004, at the beginning of the study period,
1,363 (62%) of respondents were homeowners. Our first models will use this binary
indicator for homeownership—while comparing propensity score adjustments for
selectivity bias—to predict civic engagement in 2004.

The remaining models will use a multi-category indicator that measures all
possible homeownership and mobility trajectories over the two time periods. Six
categories capture homeownership status and mobility over the four-year study

period. Table 6.2 displays percentages for these six categories, as follows: owners who did not move during the study (44%), owners who moved (13%), owners who became renters (4%), renters who did not move (14%), renters who moved (18%), and renters who became homeowners (7%). By 2007, 146 of the renters had become homeowners and 97 of the original owners had returned to renting, resulting in 1,412 (64%) homeowners in the second time period.

Using these measurements, we differentiate between homeownership status and residential mobility effects on the two civic engagement outcomes. Additionally, we include covariates that could be related to homeownership, mobility, and civic engagement. Specifically, all of our models include the following control variables: age, race, marital status, income, employment status, gender, and education.[4] We include age because older people are both more likely to be homeowners (Mingche 1977) and more likely to be involved in civic activities (Putnam 2000). We include race because it is also correlated with both homeownership and civic engagement: Minority families are more likely to rent instead of own, especially in urban communities (Massey 1990), and they are less likely to participate in instrumental forms of civic engagement (Wilson 1987). We include marital status because married couples are much more likely to own homes than single people (Townsend 2002) and are also more likely to participate in voluntary associations (Schofer & Fourcade-Gourinchas 2001). Income is correlated with homeownership, and the household debt-to-income ratio affects whether someone can obtain a mortgage. Income is also correlated with civic engagement: People with higher incomes are more likely to get involved in their communities (Verba et al. 1995). Likewise, employment status affects both one's ability to purchase a home and one's likelihood of participating in civic activities, although findings have been mixed on the nature of the latter relationship.[5] Finally, we control for both gender and level of education. Prior research has found that women participate in voluntary associations more frequently than men (Smith 1994) and that people with advanced education are more likely to be politically active (Verba et al. 1995).

We include additional control variables that could predict both homeownership and civic engagement: number of adults in the home, number of children in the home, car ownership, and neighborhood disadvantage. Family composition (i.e., the number of minors and adults in the home) likely has an impact on the time a respondent has available to participate in civic activities. The variable indicating car ownership not only measures economic status but also addresses the fact that those with personal transportation can more easily attend gatherings and meetings.[6] Finally, we control for neighborhood conditions by including an index score measuring concentrated neighborhood disadvantage (Sampson et al. 2002; Sampson & Raudenbush 1999).[7] This score represents the presence of concentrated social and economic disadvantage within neighborhoods, a factor that may influence whether or not residents elect to join neighborhood-based community groups.

Results

Our first two models predict instrumental and expressive civic engagement in the initial year of measurement, 2004. We first compare results that do not model the homeownership decision explicitly to those that do address selectivity using three kinds of propensity score analyses. In later models, we add residential stability to the analysis by creating six categories of homeownership status and mobility through the second year of measurement, 2007. We assess how the effects of homeownership and mobility interact over time in order to understand how changes in residence can affect a person's civic engagement.

Civic Engagement at Baseline

Our first models indicate that homeownership is positively associated with instrumental engagement across the four samples (Table 6.3). In the unmatched data, homeowners are more than twice as likely as renters to belong to a neighborhood-based group. This effect holds and actually increases in magnitude across the three matched samples. The results show that the homeownership effect on odds ratios increases from 2.13 in the unmatched data to 2.76, 2.99, and 3.24, respectively, following the three matches of renters to owners. Thus, all four of these analyses indicate that homeownership, compared to renting, has a statistically significant positive effect on instrumental civic engagement. In contrast, there is no homeownership effect on expressive engagement. These null results hold across all four models shown in Table 6.4. Together, results for these civic engagement outcomes provide consistent results within outcomes, across several different matching techniques. As in our chapter on financial stress, this consistency gives confidence that our results are not peculiar to a particular matching technique. Substantively, these models shows that owners are no more or less likely than comparable renters to report socializing with their neighbors, but homeowners are more likely to belong to goal-oriented neighborhood groups.

Other variables, such as race, age, employment, marriage, and education, are also statistically significant in these models. The only variable that is significantly related to both forms of civic engagement is race, with African Americans being more than twice as likely as whites to participate in a neighborhood group, yet this group is also 25% less likely to talk with their neighbors more than once a week. Being single, being out of the labor force, and having an advanced degree are all

TABLE 6.3

Instrumental Engagement Regressed on Homeownership (at Baseline)

	Unmatched	Match 1	Match 2	Match 3
Homeownership	2.13*	2.76*	2.99*	3.24*
Black (vs. white)	2.28*	2.46*	2.38*	2.42*
Other race	0.85	0.96	1.22	1.17
Female (vs. male)	0.95	0.96	1.20	.87
Income	1.69	1.51	1.52	0.39
Advanced degree (vs. high school degree or less)	2.34*	3.10*	4.96*	4.46*
4-year degree	1.28	1.10	1.36	1.23
2-year degree	1.47	2.26	1.46	1.90
Some college	1.17	1.63	1.52	1.40
Employed part-time (vs. full-time)	1.59	1.43	1.10	1.16
Unemployed	1.14	0.37	0.25	0.76
Not in labor force	1.65*	1.94	2.43	1.82
Retired	2.17*	2.89*	2.48	2.34*
Single (vs. married)	1.60*	.897	1.13	0.92
Widowed	1.87	1.06	1.19	0.89
Divorced	1.18	1.02	1.19	0.88
Cohabiting	.93	1.29	1.12	0.86

Estimation: Bivariate logistic regression.

Table displays coefficients from unmatched data and three different techniques that match renters to homeowners—in order to minimize selectivity bias of the respondent's decision to own or rent the home—as follows: unmatched data ($N = 1,813$), match 1 ($N = 688$) is a nearest neighbor within-caliper match, Match 2 ($N = 512$) is a Mahalanobis with propensity score, Match 3 ($N = 1,813$) uses propensity score weighting.

Model specification also controls for additional household demographics (age, household size, and car ownership) as well as neighborhood concentrated disadvantage and population density.

*Result is statistically significant ($p < 0.05$).

factors that are associated with a greater likelihood of being engaged in one's community in some of the models. No control variables other than race were significant predictors of socializing frequently with neighbors (or not, as was the case in the model). To focus the presentation on the homeownership effect, we suppress some of these estimates in Tables 6.3 and 6.4.

While our models suggest an association between homeownership and neighborhood group membership while adjusting for selectivity bias, these results do not fully address the question of causality, particularly over time. It may be that

TABLE 6.4

Expressive Engagement Regressed on Homeownership (at Baseline)

	Unmatched	Match 1	Match 2	Match 3
Homeownership	1.07	1.15	.98	1.03
Black (vs. white)	0.75*	0.74	0.80	.52*
Other race (vs. white)	0.92	1.17	1.28	1.22
Female (vs. male)	0.98	0.91	0.82	0.83
Income	1.06	1.70	2.13	0.49
Advanced degree (vs. high school degree or less)	0.89	0.86	0.80	1.68
4-year degree	1.03	0.90	0.98	1.48
2-year degree	0.93	1.11	0.95	0.55
Some college	1.03	0.72	0.65	1.08
Employed part-time (vs. full-time)	1.08	0.80	0.38	0.72
Unemployed	1.38	1.65	1.56	1.09
Not in labor force	1.10	1.22	1.64	1.23
Retired	1.06	1.40	1.33	0.89
Single (vs. married)	1.10	1.32	0.99	0.82
Widowed	1.14	3.03*	1.12	.072
Divorced	1.12	1.84*	1.27	1.14
Cohabiting	1.02	1.80*	1.55	1.48

Estimation: Bivariate logistic regression.

Table displays coefficients from unmatched data and three different techniques that match renters to homeowners—in order to minimize selectivity bias of the respondent's decision to own or rent the home—as follows: unmatched data ($N = 1,813$), Match 1 ($N = 688$) is a nearest neighbor within-caliper match, Match 2 ($N = 512$) is a Mahalanobis with propensity score, Match 3 ($N = 1,813$) uses propensity score weighting.

Model specification also controls for additional household demographics (age, household size, and car ownership) as well as neighborhood concentrated disadvantage and population density.

*Result is statistically significant ($p < 0.05$).

homeownership leads people to get involved in neighborhood groups, but it also may be that homeowners were also more involved in their communities as renters, prior to buying a house. We test for this possibility on the baseline 2004 outcomes by using a model that combines changes in homeownership status and mobility over time. The reason we do this is to consider how those homeowners who later moved compare—at baseline—to those homeowners who did not. Thus, this approach is a strategy that we use to consider how selectivity may affect home-ownership status and mobility over time.

TABLE 6.5

Civic Engagement Regressed on Homeownership and Mobility

	Instrumental: Neighborhood Group Participation	Expressive: Talk to Neighbors Weekly
Owner who does not move[1]	1.65*	0.95
Renter who becomes owner[1]	0.71	0.84
Owner who becomes renter[1]	0.79	1.28
Owner who moves[1]	1.54	0.90
Renter who moves[1]	0.57*	0.87

Sample size is 1,813. Respondents participated in both the 2004 and 2007 surveys.

Estimation: Bivariate logistic regressions of outcomes measured in the first year, 2004. Therefore, the columns showing "Both Years" contain a 2004 outcome that was measured *before* the 2007 measurement of the homeownership and mobility interaction. This temporal violation is intentional in order to assess group selectivity; that is, the approach allows evaluation of how first-year engagement compares across groups.

[1]Reference category is "renter who did not move."

Table displays odds ratios.

Model specification controls for household demographics (gender, age, race, marital/partner status, household size, income, employment, education, and car ownership) as well as neighborhood characteristics (neighborhood concentrated disadvantage and population density). We omit these variables from this table to focus the presentation on the interaction of homeownership status and mobility.

*Result is statistically significant ($p < 0.05$).

Results are shown in Table 6.5. The results indicate that homeownership status and mobility were *not* significant predictors of baseline expressive engagement. This result suggests that potential plans and considerations—in the respondent's mind—that might be associated with later decisions to move or purchase a home do not appear to be associated with the frequency of talking to neighbors. However, this analysis does reveal two important findings around instrumental, or goal-oriented, civic engagement. First, homeowners who did not move were more likely to be involved in a neighborhood group from the outset than renters who did not move. One possible explanation, which we discuss in the next chapter on homeownership and social capital, is that even when renters do not plan to move, others in the community still see them as transient residents and therefore do not seek their involvement in neighborhood groups.

The second important finding in Table 6.5 is that renters who moved during the study period were significantly *less* likely than renters who did not move to be involved in a neighborhood group, even prior to moving. This finding suggests that renters who anticipate that they will be moving in the future are less likely to get involved in a neighborhood group than more stable renters, as they do not plan on remaining in the neighborhood for a long time. Alternatively, it may be the case that people who are not involved in a neighborhood group feel less attached to the area and are therefore more likely to move away.

Taken together, these findings for the baseline outcomes suggest a complex relationship between homeownership status, mobility, and neighborhood group membership. The effects we observe at baseline may stem from a combination of sources—both those inherent to homeownership and those that have to do with residential stability. To understand more about this combination of factors, we next examine civic engagement outcomes at the second and final measurement, in 2007.

Civic Engagement over Time

Thus far, the models have identified baseline effects for homeownership status and mobility for instrumental engagement only; no association has been found with expressive engagement. Next we consider these factors over time. The civic engagement outcomes are now measured at the later time, in 2007. The major independent variables combine homeownership status and mobility between 2004 and 2007.

In Table 6.6, we model the full sample of respondents who participated in both the 2004 and 2007 surveys ($N = 1,813$). Note that each of these models includes the

TABLE 6.6

Civic Engagement Regressed on Homeownership and Mobility (at Follow-Up)

	Instrumental: Neighborhood Group Participation	Expressive: Talk to Neighbors Weekly
Owner who does not move[1]	1.35	0.70*
Renter who becomes owner[1]	2.80*	0.93
Owner who becomes renter[1]	0.60	0.75
Owner who moves[1]	1.50	0.61*
Renter who moves[1]	0.69	0.60*
Baseline control (instrumental)	6.61*	
Baseline control (expressive)		2.37*

Sample size is 1,813.

Estimation: Bivariate logistic regressions of two types of civic engagement: instrumental and expressive.

Table displays odds ratios. Model specification controls for household demographics (gender, age, race, marital/partner status, household size, income, employment, education, and car ownership) as well as neighborhood characteristics (neighborhood concentrated disadvantage and population density). We omit these variables from this table to focus the presentation on testing the interaction over time of homeownership status and mobility.

[1]Reference category is "renter who did not move."

*Result is statistically significant ($p < 0.05$).

respondent's corresponding level of civic engagement at baseline, 2004. By includ-ing this first-year measure, the model results estimate the changes in civic engage-ment over time. As expected, both of these baseline measures of civic engagement in 2004 are the strongest predictors of civic engagement in 2007.

The key findings in Table 6.6 concern the six-category indicator that tracks homeownership status and mobility over time. Compared to the reference group of renters who did not move, those respondents who became homeowners over the four-year study period were 2.80 times as likely to participate in neighborhood groups. Thus, those who became homeowners during the study period were almost three times as likely to be members of a neighborhood group in 2007, despite the fact that—in the prior model—the results indicated that these same respondents were not more likely to be members of a neighborhood group before they became homeowners. This finding suggests that residential stability is important and also that homeownership either precedes or closely coincides with increased neighbor-hood involvement.

Turning to expressive engagement, results in Table 6.6 suggest effects over time for mobility. Compared to the reference group of renters who did not move, own-ers who did not move were about 30% less likely to have frequent conversations with neighbors. A similar pattern is found for respondents who moved. Compared to nonmoving renters, both groups of movers are about 40% less likely to have frequent conversations with neighbors. Thus, this model provides evidence that, even more than residential stability, homeownership itself predicted expressive civic engagement (or a lack thereof).

Given these findings, we analyzed whether entering homeownership might be a catalyst for civic engagement. We know that people who were homeown-ers throughout the study were less engaged, but what about people who became homeowners? Due to the strong relationship between group membership in 2004 and the 2007 outcome, we reran the models on a subsample that consisted of only those respondents who did *not* participate in either form of civic engagement in 2004. By subsetting the data in this way, we estimate how civic engagement *increased* over time as a result of homeownership status and mobility. Table 6.7 presents the results.

Our analysis reveals that renters who became homeowners *and* who were not members of any neighborhood group in 2004 were over three times more likely to have joined a neighborhood group by 2007 when compared with the nonmoving rent-ers who did not belong to groups in 2004. The effect is similar for homeowners who relocated. Just as buying a home may prompt renters to increase their neighborhood involvement, moving to a new community seems to have done the same for estab-lished homeowners. These findings indicate that homeownership can act as a catalyst for increased civic engagement, especially when buying *and* moving to a home.

TABLE 6.7

Changes in Civic Engagement—Nonparticipants (at Baseline) Regressed on Homeownership and Mobility (at Follow-Up)

	Instrumental: Neighborhood Group Participation	Expressive: Talk to Neighbors Weekly
Owner who does not move[1]	1.45	0.70*
Renter who becomes owner[1]	4.24*	0.93
Owner who becomes renter[1]	0.81	0.75
Owner who moves[1]	2.63*	0.61*
Renter who moves[1]	0.80	0.60*

Sample size is 1,480 (instrumental), 928 (expressive).

Estimation: Bivariate logistic regressions of two types of civic engagement: instrumental and expressive.

Table displays odds ratios. Model specification controls for household demographics (gender, age, race, marital/partner status, household size, income, employment, education, and car ownership) as well as neighborhood characteristics (neighborhood concentrated disadvantage and population density). We omit these variables from this table to focus the presentation on testing the interaction over time of homeownership status and mobility.

[1]Reference category is "renter who did not move."

*Result is statistically significant ($p < .05$).

Our analysis has three primary findings: (1) both homeownership and residential stability do, indeed, have an impact on household civic engagement; (2) instrumental and expressive engagement outcomes are not tied together and, while homeowners may be more likely to engage in instrumental, or goal-seeking, activities, they are not more likely to engage in expressive activities and are, in fact, less likely to talk to their neighbors; and (3) our results differed according to mobility.

Conclusion

Based on this analysis, we conclude that an understanding of the relationship between homeownership and civic engagement requires a consideration of both ownership itself and mobility patterns. Additionally, it requires making a distinction between types of civic engagement. While homeownership predicts involvement in neighborhood organizations, this effect differs in meaningful ways depending on patterns of residential mobility. Renters who moved and continued renting were less likely to get involved in local groups than renters who did not move. However, homeowners who moved were not less likely to get involved compared to homeowners who did not move. Renters who became homeowners saw an increase in their likelihood of involvement, particularly if they were not involved prior to buying a home. Importantly, contrary to Putnam's contention, we find no evidence to support the view that homeownership leads to apathy or disengagement from instrumental forms of civic participation.

Our research findings concerning expressive civic engagement were surprising. In the 2004 data, there is no association between homeownership and whether a respondent has frequent conversations with neighbors. However, we found that in 2007 homeowners are less likely than renters who did not move to have regular conversations with their neighbors. This outcome was not predicted by any of the three explanations we tested, indicating that the mechanisms that can explain instrumental civic engagement did a poor job of explaining expressive civic engagement. One possible contributing factor that requires additional research is dwelling type: It might be that renters are more likely to live in multifamily housing units that facilitate regular interactions with neighbors more effectively than single-family detached homes do. We explore this possibility in the final chapter.

Our research also indicates the importance of considering mobility when examining causes of civic engagement, and in particular when seeking to explain instrumental civic engagement. Our findings indicate that homeowners and renters are affected differently by residential mobility. For homeowners, moving may prompt them to become more involved in neighborhood groups as a way to integrate into a new community. Renters who move (and continue to rent), however, are less likely to turn to civic participation as a way to build new social networks. This may be indicative of overall differences in long-term mobility patterns and the frequency with which renters move compared to homeowners. The findings may also stem from different expectations that neighborhood residents have of their homeowner and renter neighbors: Residents may, rightly or wrongly, expect that renters will move more often, and they will therefore be less inclined to solicit renters' participation in neighborhood groups.

Our analysis leads us to conclude that entry into homeownership can be a catalyst for increased instrumental civic engagement, but it may actually be negatively related to the likelihood of people talking with their neighbors. We discovered that renters who became homeowners were not more involved in their neighborhoods than other renters *prior to* purchasing a home, but their likelihood of such involvement increased *after* they purchased a home. This is particularly the case for renters who were not active in local groups prior to homeownership; for these renters, the likelihood of such participation increases fourfold after they buy a home. Similarly, homeowners who became renters during the study period were no more or less likely to be involved in neighborhood groups than people who had never been homeowners. Overall, our findings suggest that increasing access to homeownership can help foster a more vibrant, goal-oriented civic life in lower-income neighborhoods.

Notes

1. We model the outcome variable from an earlier point in time than the independent variables in order to evaluate whether the treatment and control groups differed on the outcome of interest prior to the intervention (purchasing a home). This analytic strategy reveals whether people who became homeowners during the study period were more involved in local organizations *prior to* purchasing a home.

2. At both time points, respondents were asked, "Do you participate in any neighborhood groups?" We use a dichotomous indicator variable coded 1 if a respondent reports participating in such a group and 0 if he or she does not.

3. Respondents were asked "In the past month, how many times have you had a conversation with a neighbor? Would you say never, once or twice, once a week or less, or more than once a week?" We coded respondents as 1 if they reported having conversations with a neighbor more than once a week, 0 if they did not.

4. Age is measured as a continuous variable. To correct for the skewed distribution of age, it is transformed to $1/\sqrt{\text{age}}$ in the regression models. Race is measured using three indicator variables: white, black, and other race. The reference category is white. Marital status is measured using the categories married, cohabiting, divorced, widowed, or single. The reference category is married. We control for income using a continuous measure of total household annual income in $10,000's. Employment status is measured using indicator variables for employed full-time, employed part-time, involuntarily unemployed, retired, and not in the paid labor force. The reference category in all models is "employed full-time." Therefore, we include an indicator variable for gender coded 1 for female and 0 for male. Because cases in which a proxy household member was interviewed were excluded from this analysis, there is no change in the gender distribution of the sample over time. Education is measured using indicator variables for the highest level of education obtained by the respondent: high school degree or less, some college, two-year college degree, four-year college degree, and advanced/professional degree. The reference category is "high school degree or less."

5. Some research has found that full-time workers are less likely to participate in voluntary activities (Burr, Caro, & Moorhead 2002), while others have concluded that retirees participate less (Glaesar, Laibson, & Sacerdote 2000).

6. While most respondents do have at least one car in 2004, there was an 11% decline in car ownership by 2007. Nonetheless, the vast majority of respondents are car owners.

7. This score is calculated based on the census tract percentages of households below the poverty line, unemployed adults, single-parent households, and families receiving public assistance. These four values are transformed to z-scores and then averaged.

7 Social Capital

AFTER DISCUSSING THE physical and mental health associations with homeownership and the correlations between local voting participation, goal-oriented civic engagement, and homeownership, we introduce more abstract concepts: social capital and collective efficacy. Both concepts focus on an individual's relationships and perceptions about others. Relationships can facilitate employment opportunities, provide emotional support, and even lead to financial support. *Social capital* is a term used by many researchers to refer to a person's network of relationships and to the "features of social life—networks, norms, and trust—that enable people to act together more effectively to pursue their goals" (Putnam 1996, pp. 664–665).

In this chapter, we analyze how homeownership relates to social capital overall and within neighborhoods. We measure social capital as access to resources rather than social networks per se. We continue to address methodological challenges related to selection bias in order to untangle key questions about causal relations. Namely, could differences in social capital be related to factors associated with homeownership, such as income or residential stability, instead of homeownership itself? Our research questions follow: Do homeowners have greater levels of social capital resources than renters? What role does residential stability play in the accumulation of social capital? And, lastly, does participation in neighborhood groups generate social capital?

Background

Social capital provides a way to understand how social networks link to important social outcomes (Lin, Cook, & Burt 2001; Van Der Gaag & Snijders 2005). In the flurry of research that surrounded the publication of *Bowling Alone* (Putnam 2001), a major exploration of social capital in the United States, the idea of social capital has been employed to explain everything from positive individual outcomes such as career advancement (Seibert, Kraimer, & Liden 2001) to positive organizational and city-level outcomes such as technology adoption (Frank, Zhao, & Borman 2004) and reductions in crime rates (Messner, Baumer, & Rosenfeld 2004). Social capital is believed to lead to positive outcomes from the individual to the national level.

Despite the purported benefits of social capital, many scholars believe that Americans have suffered from a serious decline in civic engagement and social capital over time. Putnam, for one, argues that "the weight of available evidence confirms that Americans today are significantly less engaged with their communities than was true a generation ago" and finds that "since 1965 time spent on informal socializing and visiting is down (perhaps by one-quarter) and time devoted to clubs and organizations is down even more sharply (by roughly half)" (Putnam 1995, p. 666). The decline of social capital and social networks, in Putnam's view, poses a fundamental threat to democratic governance.

There are competing hypotheses about why social capital in America has declined since the 1960s. Putnam argues that the culprit may be television: "TV watching comes at the expense of nearly every social activity outside the home, especially social gatherings and informal conversations. TV viewers are homebodies [and] television privatizes our leisure time" (Putnam 1995, p. 679). Given that *Bowling Alone* was published in 2001, it is likely that today Putnam would argue that computers, the internet, and social media, alongside television, have fundamentally changed the way Americans relate to one another. Interestingly, Putnam explicitly rejects certain hypotheses based on his research: He concludes that factors such as residential mobility, changes in marriage and family life, the changing role of women, and suburbanization are *not* the causes of the decline.

Other researchers contend that Putnam fails to consider macroeconomic changes. For instance, Skocpol argues that "if we want to repair civil society, we must first and foremost revitalize political democracy. The sway of money in politics will have to be curtailed, and privileged Americans will have to join their fellow citizens in broad civic endeavors. Reestablishing local voluntary groups alone will not suffice" (Skocpol 1996, p. 25). Whatever the cause of this decline, researchers agree that social capital is an important element of a functioning and healthy democracy. As Putnam writes in *Bowling Alone*, "What is at stake is not merely warm, cuddly feelings or frissons of community pride. [There is] hard evidence that our schools and neighborhoods don't work so well when community bonds slacken, that our economy, our democracy, and even our health and happiness depend on adequate stocks of social capital" (Putnam 2000).

While considerable research over the past 50 years has sought to document the benefits of social capital, fewer studies have explored its origins (Glaeser 2001; Glaeser & Sacerdote 2000). It is important to understand how social capital is built in order to understand how it might be cultivated, maintained, or strengthened. Thus, in our analysis, we attempt to isolate one possible source of social capital: homeownership. Before introducing our analysis, we discuss existing research on the connection between social capital and homeownership.

Social Capital and Homeownership

Social capital has been studied as both an individual (Van Der Gaag & Snijders 2005) and a collective (Bourdieu 1977) attribute; it is something that a single person can have and also something that a group or society can have. For the purpose of this research, we focus on individual social capital, defined as an individual's social network connections that are potential locations for exchange relationships (Burt, Cook, & Lin 2001). However, we expand on this idea by including measures of access to resources within these social networks (Van Der Gaag & Snijders 2005). The stipulation that network ties must have the potential to transmit resources is an important one, so in this analysis we define social capital explicitly as access to resources. Within this framework, we assume that people are aware of how their relationships may be beneficial in the future (Portes 2000). Just as a financial investment must yield dividends in order to produce wealth, a social network must yield an exchange of resources in order to influence social capital.

Social "resources" can be used to achieve an objective but are only temporarily accessed because they require connections with others (Lin 1999). Because social resources are borrowed rather than given, at least semiregular interaction is needed to maintain social capital resource connections (Son & Lin 2008). This means that for a friend, neighbor, or colleague to put you in touch with another person, it is important to continue to put time into the relationship. Thus, because homeownership offers a stable connection with one's neighbors, we ask whether homeownership is associated with higher social capital.

Research has shown that homeowners are more involved in their communities than their renter counterparts (Aaronson 2000; Dietz & Haurin 2003; Rossi & Weber 1996). However, it is not clear whether this occurs by choice or because there are fewer opportunities for renters to participate in neighborhood activities and organizations. In either case, neighborhoods with higher rates of homeownership have demonstrated "relatively high participation in local political activities and organizations, relatively high rates of voting, and [high rates of participation in] activities such as neighborhood crime watch, local school parent-teacher organizations, and other local volunteer actions" (Haurin, Dietz, & Weinberg 2002, p. 24). Indeed, we have seen this in the prior chapters of this book as well. Together, this research suggests that homeowners are more likely than renters to develop their social capital through neighborhood involvement.

When examining homeownership's potential role in developing and retaining relationships that yield social capital, it is important to consider existing theories. To understand which factors might connect homeownership with social capital, we have identified three potential influences: opportunity structures, which facilitate social interaction; place attachment, which fosters feelings of social cohesion; and residential stability, which affects expectations of reciprocity. We examine each of these factors here.

First, to acquire social capital, a person must have an opportunity to build a relationship via an opportunity structure that puts him or her in regular contact with others who have resources (Van De Bunt 1999). By "opportunity structure," we mean a social space that facilitates routine interaction with others. In a conceptual article developing these ideas, Rohe and colleagues (2002) make explicit this link between homeownership and opportunity structures. They make a distinction between the structural opportunities available in a given metropolitan area and the perceived opportunities of individuals. More specifically, they conceive of an "opportunity set" within individuals that consists of knowledge and assessments of broader structural opportunities. In this context, homeownership is seen as potentially influencing these opportunity sets of individuals through three mechanisms: wealth creation, improved health, and positive youth behaviors. Homeownership achieves these goals partly through the physical location of the dwelling as it is situated within the neighborhood, thus facilitating social interaction with others.

Perhaps the most common example of a social space that facilitates routine interaction with others is the workplace: People who share a common workplace interact with each other and often form ties that build social capital (Granovetter 1973). These workplace ties are weak in comparison to family ties or close friendships, however, since once people leave the workplace, they often cease having regular contact with their former coworkers.

Like a workplace, homeownership facilitates regular interactions within a neighborhood, and it thereby opens up opportunities for the acquisition of social capital. Regardless of whether this is an individual choice or a structural constraint—some groups may prohibit or discourage renters from joining or even require all homeowners to join without requiring any regular interaction—homeowners' greater participation in neighborhood groups often provides an opportunity to form new social ties because it puts them in at least semiregular contact with others in the neighborhood.

> It is important to learn how to fix things yourself, if possible. Talk to friends who know how to fix houses and learn from them.

The second factor that may link homeownership to the development of social capital is place attachment. Owning a home often translates into the sense of owning part of a neighborhood, and a homeowner's feelings of commitment to the home can generate feelings of commitment to the neighborhood that, in turn, can encourage interactions with neighbors. Brown and colleagues (2003) term this phenomenon "place attachment"—a sense of commitment to the home and those in the immediate neighborhood. Overall, place attachment is stronger for homeowners and long-term renters than for shorter-term residents. Woldoff (2002) found that the strongest predictor of place attachment is not the characteristics of a place but, rather, whether the subject is a homeowner. Thus, homeownership can create a strong attachment to one's home and neighborhood, and this attachment may lead to more interaction with neighbors.

The third factor affecting the development of social capital among homeowners is anticipated mobility or residential stability, which in turn affects expectations of reciprocity. Not all people within a given neighborhood will actually build relationships with each other, just as not all coworkers in a given workplace interact on a regular basis. When selecting others to connect with, people consider the potential long-term costs and benefits (Van Der Gaag & Snijders 2005). Homeowners and renters may be similarly motivated to form ties to their neighbors, but residents may see ties to homeowners as more valuable because such relationships are expected to last longer. We argue that both homeowners and renters are less likely to seek out social ties with renters because—correctly or not—renters are viewed as temporary residents. Homeownership implies permanence and residential stability, while renting implies mobility and residential instability (Coffé 2009).

While expectations of mobility can affect a renter's ability to form new social ties in a neighborhood, actual mobility can make it difficult for renters to sustain existing social ties. The CAPS data used in this study indicate that, over a four-year period, twice as many renters as homeowners moved. This finding is consistent

> Once you sign that piece of paper you are locked in.
> —Homeowner

with other research that has found strong correlations between housing status and mobility. Prior studies have shown that, when controlling for economic conditions and household wealth, expected mobility within three to five years is the strongest predictor of whether a family elects to rent or purchase a home (Boehm 1981; Henderson & Ioannides 1989). Even homeowners who live in neighborhoods with visible signs of disorder are more likely relative to renters to stay in their homes and work to improve their neighborhoods rather than move (Lee, Oropesa, & Kanan 1994). Several studies have found that communities with higher in-migration and out-migration have lower levels of social capital (Coffé 2009; Coffé & Geys 2006). Mobility is, therefore, a double-edged sword for renters: Neighbors are less likely to form ties with them due to expectations of mobility, and renters have a harder time retaining ties when they do, in fact, move.

Previous research has provided us with a strong foundation with which to think about our two primary research questions: whether homeownership is associated with greater levels of (1) social capital overall and (2) social capital within one's neighborhood. Relying on three explanations about social capital at the individual scale—opportunity structures, place attachment, and anticipated mobility—we undertake the following analysis.

Analysis

This analysis considers whether homeownership predicts overall and neighborhood-specific social capital. Specifically, our analyses seek to answer the following three questions: Do homeowners have greater levels of social capital resources than renters? What role does residential stability play in the accumulation of social capital? And does participation in neighborhood groups generate social capital? To evaluate these questions, we develop models that predict a person's social capital resources, both in general and within his or her neighborhood. Below, we detail our definitions and measurements of these concepts before unveiling our results.

Past research on social capital has been limited because most studies have tended to measure, or operationalize, social capital as the number of one's group affiliations or the number of one's network ties to others (Glaeser, Laibson, & Sacerdote 2002). It is true that people with larger social networks have more opportunities to gain social capital. However, it is more precise, but also more difficult, to measure the actual resources a person can access through his or her network, rather than merely to measure the number of network ties, which may or may not contain social resources available for exchange. Thus, our analysis looks at the specific resources to which people have access through their social networks, rather than looking only at the size of those networks.

We measure access to these resources using a "resource generator" survey that collects information on how many people a respondent knows who could provide a given resource (Van Der Gaag & Snijders 2005).[1] We differentiate between an individual's overall social capital and the social capital connected with his or her neighborhood by asking whether any of the identified social resources actually live in his or her neighborhood. If homeownership generates social capital, we would expect homeowners to have more overall social capital resources overall *and* more resources within their actual neighborhoods. If homeownership only influences the social capital in one's own area, we expect homeowners to know more people in their neighborhoods with resources but not more people in general.

Our analysis is constructed based on specific resources that are meaningful to the study population. For example, it would make little sense to ask respondents in our study whether they know someone who could help them learn Martian, or any other skill with little value within our study population. We therefore selected social resources that are not homeowner-specific but that are relevant more generally to low- and moderate-income Americans. The items were introduced by telling respondents that the questions would ask them about people who live outside their home who could offer specific skills or resources if needed, without expecting to get paid for their services. For example, the first question stated, "Other than people who live with you, how many people do you know who would help you move to a new home?" Seven more items were also presented, asking how many people respondents knew who (1) would bring them food or medicine if they were sick, (2) have contacts in the media, (3) are politically active, (4) would give good advice for handling stress, (5) are good with computers, (6) could help them find a job, and (7) would lend them $500 if they needed it. Each of these items also included a follow-up question that asked whether any of the people indicated by the respondents lived in the neighborhood.

Using responses to these questions, we created measures for overall and neighborhood social capital. Items were coded as 1 if the respondent knew anyone would help; otherwise 0. Thus, we used a binary indicator when summing items in both scales. In this way, the scales for overall and neighborhood-specific social capital were created in similar ways and both ranged from 0 to 8. Overall social capital is the sum of resources a person reports anywhere and neighborhood-specific social capital is the sum of resources to which a person has access within his or her neighborhood.

TABLE 7.1

Social Capital—Descriptive Statistics

Variable	Mean	Std. Dev.	Min	Max
Social capital resources	6.04	1.71	0	8
Neighborhood social capital	2.46	2.28	0	8
Neighborhood concentrated disadvantage	0.04	0.57	−0.78	4.33
Neighborhood concentrated immigration	−0.12	0.76	−0.69	4.74
Neighborhood residential stability	−0.07	0.52	−5.57	1.27
Neighborhood concentrated affluence	−0.24	0.74	−1.52	3.10

$N = 2,902$

Descriptive statistics for these and other key variables are presented in Table 7.1. The mean score on the resource generator for overall social capital is 6.04, indicating that, on average, our respondents report knowing at least one person who could help them with six of the eight resources we identified. The mean score for neighborhood-specific resources is much lower, at 2.46. These results indicate that, within their neighborhoods, our survey respondents report substantially fewer contacts who could provide resources than in a more general context.

Additionally, we were interested in whether social capital results are related to homeownership itself or, rather, to residential stability. We analyzed time in residence in order to test whether any apparent homeownership effects can be explained away by including a measure of how long a respondent has lived in his or her neighborhood. We also used modeling techniques that account for self-selection into homeownership. Some researchers have suggested that the mechanism through which homeownership leads to social benefits is by reducing residential mobility (Boehm 1981; Henderson & Ioannides 1989). Alternatively, other studies have concluded that homeownership leads to higher social capital even when controlling for mobility. Robert Putnam also questions residential stability as the primary cause of the decreases of social capital and engagement more broadly, writing that "Evidence fully exonerates residential mobility from any responsibility for our fading civic engagement" (Coffé 2009; Coffé & Geys 2006; Putnam 1995, p. 669). We attempt to study these links between homeownership, residential stability, and social capital with our analysis.

Many of the studies that investigate the role of residential stability in linking homeownership to social capital have not differentiated between moving from one city to another (inter-metropolitan migration) and moving from one house to another within the same community (intra-metropolitan mobility). This is a crucial distinction, because moving within the same area does not lead to a loss of contacts, relationships, or resources in one's area. In this study, we measure mobility across, rather than within, neighborhoods. Thus, with our measure of mobility, we assess how long a respondent has lived within the same neighborhood.[2]

Lastly, we test whether participation in a neighborhood organization mediates the relationship between homeownership and social capital. This potential mediator, neighborhood group participation, is the same measure of instrumental civic engagement that we examined in the prior chapter. If homeowners are more likely to participate in neighborhood groups, then this type of instrumental engagement with the community could be an important mechanism through which owners expand their social capital ties to others in their communities. We therefore include an indicator for whether or not a respondent participates in a neighborhood group. Relying on this measurement and the others listed above, we present our results.

Results

Our analysis is split into two outcomes, one predicting overall social capital and one predicting neighborhood-specific social capital. We use two models for each of these outcomes. Models 1 and 3 include a full set of demographic and neighborhood variables. Models 2 and 4 are "trimmed" to include only those variables that are statistically significant. We trimmed the nonsignificant covariates to improve how well the model fits the data. In addition, this second model includes a potential mediator, neighborhood group participation, the same measure for instrumental civic engagement that we explored in the last chapter. Having outlined this strategy, next we review the findings.

Overall Social Capital

Results for all four of these models are displayed in Table 7.2. Our first analysis predicts *overall* social capital, measured as how many people one knows who could help with certain activities, with two separate models. Models 1 and 2 both show that homeownership is a statistically significant predictor of overall social capital. Compared to similar renters, homeowners score 0.88 higher on the eight-point scale for overall social capital, controlling for all else.

TABLE 7.2

Social Capital Regressed on Homeownership, Residential Mobility, and Neighborhood

Predictors	Overall Social Capital		In the Neighborhood	
	Model 1	Model 2	Model 3	Model 4
Homeowner	0.89*	0.88*	0.75	1.11*
Age 30–39 (vs. under 30)	−0.19	−0.19	−0.07	−0.15
40–49	−0.21	−0.23*	0.31	0.20
50–59	−0.43*	−0.47*	0.17	0.03
60–69	−0.49*	−0.59*	0.39	0.34
70–79	−1.22*	−1.31*	−0.47	−0.65
80+	−0.97*	−1.13*	−1.80*	−2.01*
Black (vs. white)	0.43*	0.31*	−0.03	
Hispanic	−0.56*	−0.62*	−0.17	
Other race	−0.15	−0.19	−0.35	
Cohabiting (vs. married)	−0.03	−0.03	−0.06	
Widowed	0.41	0.44*	−0.25	
Divorced/separated	0.33*	0.33*	−0.12	
Single	0.18	0.17	−0.01	
2-year degree (vs. high school diploma)	0.34*	0.35*	0.34	0.34
4-year degree	0.53*	0.51*	0.15	0.09
Advanced degree	0.76*	0.69*	0.52*	0.38*
Unemployed (vs. employed)	−0.39*	−0.44*	−0.18	
Retired	−0.42	−0.47*	0.34	
Not in labor force	−0.27	−0.29	0.17	
Relative income	0.20*	0.17*	0.17	
Child(ren) in home	−0.01		0.26*	0.25*
Lived in neighborhood less than 1 year (vs. 3 years or more)	0.10		−0.03	
Lived 1–3 years in neighborhood	0.04		−0.27	
Neighborhood disadvantage	−0.08		0.19	
Neighborhood immigration	−0.03		−0.05	
Neighborhood stability	0.04		0.08	

TABLE 7.2

Continued

Predictors	Overall Social Capital		In the Neighborhood	
	Model 1	Model 2	Model 3	Model 4
Neighborhood affluence	0.02		0.05	
Instrumental civic engagement (i.e., neighborhood group participation)		0.59*		1.04*

N = 2,902. This treatment effects model uses robust standard errors to cluster by census tract.
*Result is statistically significant (p < 0.05).

Age is significantly related to overall social capital, yet findings from Model 2 reveal no significant differences among respondents under 40. These findings suggest that age may have a threshold effect around the age of 40, because people over 40 have fewer social capital resources, and as people get older their resources decline progressively.

Models 1 and 2 also reveal race effects: Compared to whites, blacks score about one-third of a point higher on the eight-point scale for overall social capital. This is consistent with Stack's (1983) work on the social networks of lower-income black households. Interestingly, we find the opposite effect when looking at Hispanic households, which score about one-half of a point lower on the scale, indicating slightly fewer resources than whites. We speculate that this result may be because immigrants have not had the opportunity to develop extensive social networks; additionally, language barriers may limit the social networks some Hispanic families are able to develop. It is also possible that certain social resources we measure in this analysis, such as contacts in the media, are less relevant to some Hispanic families, particularly undocumented residents or recent immigrants.

Another notable finding is that being divorced is statistically significant and shows a positive relationship to social capital, meaning that divorced people have more social ties to others with useful resources. This could be because people who get divorced rely more on their social networks for assistance with things they may have previously received from their partner, like obtaining food or medicine when sick. Another possibility is that divorced respondents may spend more time socializing and therefore may have larger social networks than married or cohabiting respondents.

Higher levels of education are also associated with higher overall social capital, and the effect size increases as levels of education increase. This trend has two possible explanations. First, attending college may give one an opportunity to interact with more people and therefore expand one's social networks. Another explanation is that education is closely tied to occupation and, in turn, to occupational prestige. People with greater occupational prestige, such as doctors, may be desirable social contacts and thus others may form social ties with them intentionally. This connection between educational attainment and social capital resources merits further study, as it has not been extensively examined within low- to moderate-income populations like those represented in the CAPS sample.

Finally, looking at employment status and overall social capital, we find that only unemployed respondents differ significantly from those who are employed or those who are voluntarily out of the labor force. Being unemployed is associated with lower overall social capital resources. This is likely due to a decline in frequent interactions with coworkers.

Model 1 also tests whether residential stability is associated with higher levels of overall social capital. The variable includes a measure of residential stability that consists of categorical indicators for the amount of time lived in the neighborhood. Shorter amounts of time lived in the neighborhood are compared to three or more years, but none of these indicators are statistically significant. Time lived in the neighborhood is not associated with social capital in any of the models.

Finally, in Model 2 we include neighborhood group membership—the measure of instrumental civic engagement. We hypothesize that this variable may have an indirect effect on social capital by mediating the association between homeownership and social capital. This measure is statistically significant but accounts for only a small amount of the total homeownership effect.[3]

Neighborhood Social Capital

The second analysis uses a similar strategy to predict neighborhood-specific social resources (Models 3 and 4 in Table 7.2). In contrast to the measure of overall social capital, neighborhood-specific social capital is a measure of the number of social resources a person can access through network connections *within the neighborhood*. As in our first analysis, the specification for Model 3 includes the full set of demographic and neighborhood variables, whereas the fourth model is trimmed to include only statistically significant variables. This final model also includes the measure of neighborhood group participation.

This analysis reveals several important findings. First, homeownership does significantly predict neighborhood-specific social capital, but only in the final, trimmed estimation. Note that homeownership is not statistically significant in Model 3, which includes a larger set of demographic and neighborhood covariates. With Model 4, we trim away these nonsignificant variables and remodel while including only statistically significant predictors. This approach yields a more concise or "parsimonious" set of estimates. The results from Model 4 indicate that homeownership is a positive and statistically significant predictor of neighborhood social capital. Compared to similar renters, homeowners score more than one point higher on the eight-point scale for neighborhood social capital. This finding supports the idea that homeownership provides residents with a platform from which to connect to and interact with neighbors.

A second notable finding is that most of the sociodemographic characteristics that were predictive of social capital resources overall are *not* significant when looking at social capital within the neighborhood. The age effect is largely gone, with only those age 80 and older differing significantly from respondents under 30. While the oldest respondents have less neighborhood-specific social capital, the remaining age categories are not significant in this model. Additionally, having a child in the home is associated with more social capital resources within the neighborhood. As with the prior outcome, both residential stability and the neighborhood characteristics, such as affluence and stability, have no association with neighborhood social capital.

A third finding from Model 4 (neighborhood-based social capital) concerns a potential mediator, neighborhood group membership. This estimate is statistically significant, which suggests that it has an indirect effect and partially mediates the association between homeownership and neighborhood social capital. However, the estimate accounts for only a small amount of the total homeownership effect.[4]

These two analyses help us understand the relationship among homeownership, residential stability, group membership, and social capital. We find that homeownership is, in fact, related to higher levels of overall and neighborhood-specific social capital. Demographic factors such as age, race, marriage and cohabitation, education, and employment are important in contributing to overall social capital resources but do not have a strong association at the neighborhood level. We also find that residential stability is not influential, suggesting that the impact of homeownership on social capital comes from other pathways. One possibility is participation in neighborhood groups, which does partially mediate the effect of homeownership on social capital. Our results, taken together, indicate that home-ownership itself has a positive association with social capital overall and within the neighborhood.

Conclusion

Before we began our analysis, we asked three questions concerning homeown-ership and social capital: Do homeowners have greater levels of social capital resources than renters? What role does residential stability play in the accumula-tion of social capital? And does participation in neighborhood groups generate social capital? We summarize our findings related to each question before conclud-ing with a brief discussion of the implications of this analysis.

Our findings suggest that the answer to the first question is yes, homeowners do have greater levels of social capital than renters, even after taking into account alternative explanations. We also found that the relationship between homeown-ership and social capital remains significant even after accounting for residential mobility and neighborhood context. Lastly, the analysis indicates that participa-tion in neighborhood groups mediates social capital; neighborhood group mem-bership has a significant positive impact on social capital, but it explains only a slight amount of the higher social capital that homeowners have.

Our research contributes to an understanding of how social capital is developed by focusing on the individual in a debate that is often at the macro level. Studies of social capital have documented sociodemographic patterns in the distribution of social capital but have often failed to account for the causes of those differ-ences beyond explanations that rely on macro-level social structures. According to such studies, different groups have more or less social capital due to the oppor-tunities or disadvantages those groups face overall. Our analysis asks whether an individual-level decision to buy a home can create opportunities to gain social capital. Given that entry into homeownership is associated with higher social capi-tal among lower-income residents, future research might consider this and other individual-level catalysts.

Finally, our research suggests that homeownership does provide an opportunity for social interaction and fosters greater social involvement within neighborhoods. We conclude that, through this involvement, homeowners have opportunities to expand their social networks and interact with other members of their local com-munities. Importantly, the higher social capital of lower-income homeowners is not a result of their being less mobile, although expectations of the future mobil-ity of neighbors may make them less likely to initiate social ties. Homeownership, therefore, can provide a pathway for low- and moderate-income families to access social capital resources.

This conclusion is especially important in light of the Great Recession and associated housing market decline. Our work suggests that there are social benefits associated with policies aimed at supporting homeownership among the low- and moderate-income population. Programs such as the Hardest Hit Fund, designed to help homeowners remain in their homes during the house price declines, may not only provide a financial safety net but could also help these owners retain their relationships and social resources. Based on the findings presented in this chapter, policymakers could more fully consider the economic and the social costs and benefits of housing policies designed to support and sustain homeownership opportunities. We detail these and other policy implications in the concluding chapter of this book.

Notes

1. The advantage of using a resource generator to measure social capital is that it measures the actual resources to which a person has access through his or her social network. Alternative measures such as a name generator or position generator measure the size or prestige of one's social networks but not the resources within those networks.

2. Because we have multiple observations within metropolitan statistical areas, we obtain robust variance estimates to account for clustering at the metropolitan statistical area level (Froot 1989).

3. We used the Sobel-Goodman mediation test to determine how much of the direct effect of homeownership is mediated by the inclusion of the neighborhood group membership variable. The test indicated that the indirect effect is significant but small, accounting for only 2.7% of the total homeownership effect.

4. We ran the Sobel-Goodman mediation test and determined that 5.1% of the overall homeownership effect on neighborhood social capital is explained by neighborhood group membership.

8 Collective Efficacy and Perceived Crime

THE PREVIOUS ANALYSES in this book examine personal attitudes and behaviors such as individual health outcomes, voting participation, and social capital. In this chapter, we shift the focus to a concept called "collective efficacy" and its potential link to neighborhood crime. This concept, which reveals a willingness to work together with one's neighbors to achieve a common goal, has been associated with a reduction of violent crime in neighborhoods. Crime in neighborhoods is highly correlated with poverty and unemployment, and scholars have also linked the attitudes that make up the concept of collective efficacy to reduced crime (Sampson, Raudenbush, & Earls 1997). This link implies that collective efficacy, alongside other important factors, matters in improving quality of life for residents.

While many studies have since examined the consequences of collective efficacy and associated reductions in crime, much less is known about the antecedents—that is, the factors that lead to or enhance collective efficacy. Few, if any, policy tools have been identified as potential precursors to collective efficacy. Because homeownership is one such policy tool that could improve quality of life in neighborhoods, we first consider whether collective efficacy is associated with homeownership and, if so, whether this result is related to homeownership itself or to another related concept such as neighborhood stability.

Second, we consider whether and how homeownership is related to crime. Our dataset does not contain actual crime statistics, so we use an alternate measure, perceived crime. Our measure of perceived crime is analogous to the perceived violence measure originally tested by Sampson and colleagues (1997). Their study showed that collective efficacy is linked to reductions in perceived violence as well as actual violent crimes.

It is important to acknowledge that wide variation exists between people on many perceptions regarding their neighborhoods—perhaps most notably, residents of different neighborhoods can perceive levels of neighborhood disorder differently (Sampson & Raudenbush 2004). In contrast, there is relatively high agreement about perceptions of neighborhood crime. As Wesley K. Skogan (1990) observed, "In the case of common crime, a large body of research indicates that there *is* in fact a value consensus. People of all races and classes agree we should shun theft, violence, sexual assault, and aggression against children" (p. 5). Thus, while we realize that our measure of perceived crime is not as good as actual crime data—which we could not reliably link to the attitudes of our survey respondents—we also note that there is a good deal of agreement regarding what constitutes crime.

> Some of the neighbors are rowdy at night. Cars have been broken into. There are lots of rentals, people come and go and come and go.

In any case, our analytic focus in this chapter is to consider whether and how homeownership relates to collective efficacy theory and perceived crime. Following other chapters in this book, we first adjust for the selectivity of owning a home before evaluating the consequences of homeownership on collective efficacy processes and outcomes. More specifically, we ask: Does homeownership have a direct effect on collective efficacy, and an indirect effect, through collective efficacy, on perceived crime?

Background

Before discussing our analysis, we review the literature around the key concepts of collective efficacy (encompassing both a sense of community and a willingness to fix problems) and neighborhood crime. We then review theories about the connection between homeownership and collective efficacy before presenting our research questions and methods.

The idea of collective efficacy has been established by previous scholars. The concept is built on Bandura's theory of individual self-efficacy (2000), which refers to judgments and beliefs about how well individuals can handle particular situations. Bandura recognized an interdependence between these beliefs of individuals and those beliefs that are shared by groups of people. The shared beliefs about the ability of groups to address particular situations was called *collective efficacy*.

> The violence has increased, the past year I have heard gunshots, and at night the police were looking for people with helicopters.

The power of these shared beliefs to explain the incidence of violent crime in neighborhoods has given collective efficacy its appeal. More specifically, this concept of collective efficacy has been related to several measures of neighborhood crime. In particular, Sampson and colleagues (1997) published a seminal study of Chicago neighborhoods that linked the idea of collective efficacy to the reduction of violent crime in neighborhoods. Specifically, these researchers demonstrated that actual homicides, the likelihood of being a violent crime victim, and perceptions of violent crime are all less likely when members of neighborhoods have higher levels of collective efficacy (Sampson et al. 1997). By reducing violent crime, these findings demonstrate that collective efficacy is meaningful in terms of neighborhood-level quality of life.

Many scholars have connected violent crime to structural factors such as poverty. Some have hypothesized that the "alienation, exploitation, and dependency wrought by resource deprivation act as a centrifugal force that stymies collective efficacy" (Sampson et al. 1997, p. 919). This implies that structural factors like income inequality, poverty, and segregation make criminal activity more likely (Office of Policy Development and Research, 2016). However, the attitudes and shared beliefs that define collective efficacy have also been found to deter criminal outcomes. Thus, it is important to call attention to the caution put forth by the original researchers, who said that recognizing that "collective efficacy matters does not imply that inequalities at the neighborhood level can be neglected" (Sampson et al. 1997, p. 923).

Thus, aside from engaging with deep structural contributors to crime such as high poverty, segregation, or inequality, neighborhoods generally adopt one of two predominant strategies: one authoritative, the other participatory. Criminal behavior in neighborhoods can be mitigated in authoritative ways, such as through a formal police presence. But policing is expensive and can be controversial. Particularly in communities of color, a growing awareness of the disproportionate outcomes associated with policing has eroded community members' trust in police (Epp, Maynard-Moody, & Haider-Markel 2014). Additionally, the challenges of police work itself are dramatic; police officers often earn low-income salaries while taking great risks in highly demanding situations. In many ways, then, policing is not the ideal way for society to keep peace. Formal policing is at best a partial solution to the wide array of problems that arise in neighborhoods.

Another way to confront neighborhood crime is through the participation of the residents themselves. This is an informal approach that is less expensive and can be more effective. The informal process by which residents themselves reduce neighborhood crime—without relying on law enforcement—is called collective efficacy. In this chapter, we first review why the group process called collective efficacy is possibly the most useful, efficient, and sensible way to fix neighborhood problems. Then, we empirically explore how homeownership relates to collective efficacy processes and outcomes.

Like Sampson and colleagues (1997), we conceive of collective efficacy in neighborhoods as being characterized by two things: a sense of community and a willingness to fix problems.[1] Both aspects—one a feeling, one an action—are needed to minimize neighborhood crime; if either is missing, neighborhoods will suffer. Before discussing this interdependence, we introduce each aspect as we build a framework for how homeownership itself relates to crime reduction in neighborhoods.

Sense of community was conceived by Sarason (1974) as perceived similarity and feelings of interdependence with others. Building on Sarason's ideas, McMillan and Chavis (1986) proposed that sense of community consists of four parts: membership, influence, emotional connection, and reinforcement of needs. More specifically, sense of community was defined as "a feeling that members have of belonging, a feeling that members matter to one another and to the group, and a shared faith that members' needs will be met through their commitment to be together" (p. 9). This sense of community concept was then applied to the neighborhood context.

Traditionally, the study of neighborhoods has relied on demographic characteristics, such as a neighborhood's level of income and unemployment, or the percentage of residents in a neighborhood who have children or who identify with a racial or ethnic group. Chavis, Hogge, McMillan, and Wandersman (1986) departed from this emphasis on demographic features by assessing the feelings and experiences that residents have with their neighborhoods. These researchers designed survey questions to explicitly focus on emotional experiences as key to understanding a psychology of community. These survey questions, which we use in this chapter, formed the first index measuring sense of community. While other researchers use alternative terms such as social cohesion or place attachment, we view these concepts as being so closely related that they are indistinguishable, and, in this chapter, we generally refer to them as *sense of community*. In our analysis, we consider residents'

> Homeownership gives you a sense of security. I love it, the kids love it. It gives us a sense of community and stability.

psychological sense of community in conjunction with the more traditional structural and demographic explanations of neighborhoods.

The second aspect essential to collective efficacy is a *willingness to fix problems*. Unlike sense of community, which focuses on a feeling, this aspect involves action. More specifically, collective efficacy requires a willingness by neighbors to take positive social actions when local problems arise such as physical fighting in the street or children showing disrespect to adults. There are many ways neighbors can address such problems, but the key to this dimension is that positive steps are taken toward finding a solution. Because positive actions are taken to address specific neighborhood problems, the actions are characterized as interventions (Sampson et al. 1997).

When neighborhoods have *both* a sense of community *and* a willingness to fix problems, criminal activity is reduced (Bellair & Browning 2010). However, neighborhoods will suffer if either one of the two key elements is absent. For example, a neighborhood where people are willing to fix problems—yet without a sense of community—can become a place of distrust, fear, and paranoia. Alternatively, a neighborhood with only a sense of community—where problems are not confronted—can become a place of frustration, anger, and despair. But in those neighborhoods where a high sense of community combines with a willingness to fix problems, criminal activity is less likely and people are more likely to thrive.

> It's nice to have neighbors and own your home, but you never know who's going to move in.
>
> —Homeowner

Our goal is to consider how homeownership relates to this idea of collective efficacy. We introduce prior research that has examined how aspects of housing relate to the key concepts of sense of community and a willingness to fix problems. Then, we present two ideas about why homeownership may be associated with higher levels of collective efficacy.

Prior research has linked the first key element, sense of community, to housing and mobility. For example, household stability has been associated with sense of community in several studies, as have home equity and homeownership (Long & Perkins 2007). However, no published studies have evaluated whether the association of homeownership with sense of community persists after adjusting for the selection bias that accompanies the decision to own or rent the home.

The second component, a willingness to fix problems, has also been examined. Using data from Chicago neighborhoods, Sampson and colleagues (1997) found that housing and mobility features were predictive; specifically, homeownership was positively associated with social cohesion plus the willingness of neighbors to intervene on behalf of the common good. Time in the neighborhood and the stability of households were included as control variables. Thus, the study did assess how aspects of housing relate to collective efficacy, but it did not focus on the homeownership effect itself.

Aside from these empirical links, there are two key theoretical reasons why homeownership might relate to collective efficacy. First, because most homeowners view their homes as financial investments, they are motivated to maintain and improve their houses. Because house prices depend on local neighborhood conditions, homeowners may be more motivated to attend not only to their own houses, but also to amenities within their neighborhood. When compared to similar renters, homeowners would seem to be more financially vested in their homes and, thus, may have greater incentive to maintain and improve both their homes and neighborhoods (Dietz & Haurin 2003; Herbert & Belsky 2008; Rohe & Lindblad 2014; Rohe et al. 2000).

Second, homeowners are less mobile than renters, and this stability may increase collective efficacy. Purchasing a home carries large transaction costs and typically requires up to five years for financial returns. Even in appreciating housing markets, recent homebuyers have an incentive to stay in their home for years rather than move away from their investment. In depreciating housing markets, mobility options may be further reduced due to negative home equity and an inability to sell the home at profit. With home sale being financially undesirable, the house may constrain homeowners' option to move away from neighborhood problems, yet in this way may also motivate residents to address problems in their neighborhood. That is, instead of moving to a different neighborhood or otherwise ignoring neighborhood problems, homeowners may be more motivated than renters to confront and act upon local problems. Thus, the reduced mobility associated with homeownership may encourage homeowners to maintain and improve their neighborhood (Dietz & Haurin 2003; Herbert & Belsky 2008; Rohe & Lindblad 2014; Rohe et al. 2000).

> The neighborhood was very good, but has been going down, so I am moving, relocating. The crime is out of control. There are too many drugs, drunks, shootings, and the noise is all out of control.

Informed by existing research in this area, our primary research questions in this chapter follow: Are homeowners, indeed, more likely than similar renters to confront neighborhood problems? And is this potential association based on homeownership itself, or does it have more to do with concepts that are related to neighborhood context? Scholars agree that violent crime in neighborhoods is reduced when a sense of community combines with a willingness to fix problems, yet, surprisingly, little research investigates the policy levers that might increase these collective efficacy processes. Homeownership is one such policy tool.

Analysis

Before describing our analytic techniques, we detail our measures, including the two outcomes, collective efficacy and perceptions of crime. Initially, we describe how collective efficacy derives from two elements: sense of community and a willingness to fix problems. To understand a person's sense of community, survey respondents indicated how strongly they agreed or disagreed with statements about the neighborhood using eight of the items originally proposed by Chavis and colleagues (1986). Examples of these statements include "I feel at home in my neighborhood" and "I think my neighborhood is a good place to live." All eight items used in our analysis are shown in Table 8.1.

The second dimension of collective efficacy is the willingness to intervene on behalf of the common good. We assess this willingness to fix problems using four items originally identified by Sampson and coauthors (1997). For instance, respondents were asked, "If a fight broke out in front of your house, how likely is it that your neighbors would do something about it? Would you say it is very likely, likely, unlikely, or very unlikely?" These same response options were presented for three additional situations: children showing disrespect to an adult, children spray-painting graffiti on a local building, and a nearby fire station threatened with budget cuts. It is important to note that, for all four of these items, survey respondents were not asked about their own behavior but, rather, the behavior of their neighbors. This approach follows the original framework used by Sampson and coworkers (1997). Thus, respondent's assessments of their neighbors' willingness to "do something" about these hypothetical situations informs each indicator of willingness to fix problems. Items and descriptive statistics are shown in Table 8.1.

We use a technique called factor analysis to combine items that assess a person's sense of community or willingness to fix problems (see Table 8.1).[2] Each item is weighted differently, meaning that some items contribute more to the construct, or factor, than others. The far-right column of Table 8.1 indicates that the item "I think my neighborhood is a good place to live" contributes more than the other seven indicators to the *sense of community* factor.

Similarly, we use factor analysis to combine the two elements, sense of community and willingness to fix problems (see Table 8.1). The factor loadings for these two elements are similar, indicating that these elements contribute about equally to the collective efficacy construct. Together, sense of community and willingness to fix problems form the first key outcome, collective efficacy.

For the second key outcome, we examine perceptions of neighborhood crime. Survey participants were asked, "What do you consider to be the biggest problem

TABLE 8.1

Collective Efficacy and Perceived Crime—Descriptive Statistics

Element	Question Wording and Items	Mean	Standard Deviation	Factor Loading
Sense of Community	*Now I have a few questions about your neighborhood. Please tell me how strongly you agree or disagree with the following statements: (strongly agree = 5, strongly disagree = 1)*			1.21
	I think my neighborhood is a good place to live	3.83	0.84	1.00
	My neighbors and I want the same things from the neighborhood	3.89	0.97	.84
	I can recognize most of the people who live in my neighborhood	3.68	1.19	.76
	I feel at home in my neighborhood	4.13	0.86	.95
	I care what my neighbors think of my actions	3.57	1.18	.52
	If there is a problem in this neighborhood people who live here can get it solved	3.63	1.00	.83
	It is very important to me to live in this particular neighborhood	3.34	1.13	.94
	I expect to live in this neighborhood for a long time	3.37	1.19	.73

(continued)

TABLE 8.1

Continued Element	Question Wording and Items	Mean	Standard Deviation	Factor Loading
Willingness to Fix Problems	*I am going to describe situations that may arise in a neighborhood. Please rate how likely it is that your neighbors would do something in response to the following situations: (very likely = 4, very unlikely = 1)*			1.00
	If a fight broke out in front of your house, how likely is it that your neighbors would do something about it?	3.14	0.98	1.00
	If the fire station closest to your home was threatened with budget cuts . . .	2.94	0.88	1.08
	If children were showing disrespect to an adult . . .	2.87	0.97	1.11
	If children were spray-painting graffiti on a local building . . .	3.36	0.81	1.26

Sample of 750 households comprises 375 owners and 375 renters matched through propensity score analysis (Lindblad, Manturuk, & Quercia 2013).

in your neighborhood? Would you say crime, schools, availability of jobs, changes in the neighborhood, traffic, or some other issue?" People who said crime were coded 1 for perceived crime. Of the final matched sample of 750 respondents, 124 (16.5%) indicated that crime was the biggest problem in their neighborhood, and of these, 52 (42%) were homeowners and 72 (58%) were renters.

As measures of neighborhood context, we use census tract data to consider three indicators: population density, neighborhood disadvantage, and residential stability. We assess population density to control for potential effects of crowding. Neighborhood disadvantage is the sum of four neighborhood indicators: percent single parents, percent unemployed, percent on public assistance, and percent in poverty. Lastly, neighborhood residential stability combines the percent of occupied residences and the percent of residents who have lived in same house for five or more years.

As with all analyses in this book, we take special care to confront the challenge of selection bias in the decision to own or rent the home. Additionally, we consider a host of control variables that may influence the two major outcomes, collective efficacy and perceptions of neighborhood crime. At the household level, we adjust for the self-efficacy of individuals according to the respondents' ratings (on a four-point scale) of the ability of people like themselves to solve their neighborhood's biggest problem. Specifically, we ask the following question: "Overall, how much of a difference do you think people like you can make on [reducing crime, improving schools, unemployment, neighborhood change, traffic, etc.]," where the bracketed text is filled with the respondents' response to the previously described question, "What do you consider to be the biggest problem in your neighborhood?" We include this variable to control for the potential confound to collective efficacy that is posed by respondents' ratings of self-efficacy. We also consider the demographic background of the respondent, including age, education, race and ethnicity, marital or partner status, and the presence of children.

Results

Our analysis first examines the building blocks of collective efficacy: sense of community and willingness to fix problems. Then, we present results for the two key outcomes: collective efficacy and perceived crime. Our overall goal is to examine potential associations among homeownership, the two elements of collective efficacy, and perceived crime.

Model results indicate that there is a positive association between homeownership, sense of community, willingness to fix problems, and collective efficacy (Table 8.2). The first model shows that homeowners and older respondents both report a higher sense of community. On the five-point Likert scale indicating agreement, the sense of community score for homeowners is 0.17 higher than for comparable renters.

Homeownership is also significant in results shown for the second model, willingness to fix problems. On the four-point Likert scale indicating the likelihood that neighbors would intervene, homeowners score 0.23 higher than renters. Willingness to fix problems is also positively associated with age and the self-efficacy of the respondent, and negatively associated with the population density of the neighborhood.

After establishing that homeownership is positively associated with both sense of community and a willingness to fix problems, we combine these two elements as a single factor, collective efficacy (Model 3). As expected, this outcome is positively associated with self-efficacy. This finding confirms Bandura's (2000) point that collective efficacy is rooted in the beliefs of individuals.

TABLE 8.2

Sense of Community and Willingness to Fix Problems as Collective Efficacy
Regressed on Homeownership

	Sense of Community	+	Willingness to Fix Problems	=	Collective Efficacy
	Model 1		Model 2		Model 3, Panel A
Homeowner (compared to renter)	0.17*		0.23*		0.17*
Self-efficacy	0.05		0.06*		0.05*
Age (51 years or older)	0.17*		0.13*		0.14*
Income (relative to area median income)	−0.09		−0.00		−0.05
Neighborhood disadvantage	−0.05		0.01		−0.02
Neighborhood population density	−0.05		−0.07*		−0.05*
Neighborhood residential stability	0.04		0.07		0.05

$N = 750$. Table presents unstandardized estimates. Collective efficacy is a second-order factor measured by two first-order factors: sense of community and willingness to fix problems. All indicators are shown in Table 8.1. Model 3 has two outcomes (collective efficacy and crime perceptions) and is continued in Table 8.3.
* means statistically significant.

Note that we also control for household income, which is *not* a statistically significant predictor of any outcomes in this chapter. Nonsignificant results are also evident for race and ethnicity, education, marital or partner status, and the presence of children.[3] In fact, nearly all household characteristics are nonsignificant for two reasons. First, prior to the current analysis, we matched renters to owners in order to isolate the homeownership effect. This match neutralized much of the demographic noise in the data. Second, and more importantly, there is little theoretical reason to expect differences based on most demographic characteristics of households—that is, we see no reason to think that respondents of one particular gender or racial or ethnic group would be more inclined than those from another group to differentially assess their neighbors' willingness to "do something" about neighborhood problems.

Correspondingly, we find no effect on collective efficacy for any household demographics except age. Compared to younger respondents, those aged 51 years or older score 0.14 higher on the four-point Likert scale indicating the likelihood that their neighbors would confront problems. These results do suggest that, controlling for all else, older people may feel more attached to their neighborhoods and believe more strongly in the capacity of their neighbors to fix problems.

While most household demographics have little sway, one might expect that the social composition or conditions of the neighborhood could influence collective efficacy. Yet Table 8.2 shows that only population density is associated with collective efficacy: Those respondents who live in more densely populated areas report lower levels of collective efficacy. This finding for population density may reflect the diffusion of responsibility that can occur as group size increases; diffused responsibility can lead to a "bystander effect" in which helping behavior becomes less likely (Darley & Latane 1968). In any case, these results signal greater challenges for more densely populated neighborhoods in establishing the social processes involved in collective efficacy. Meanwhile, other neighborhood indicators in Table 8.2 are not statistically significant. Respondents' rating of the neighborhood's collective efficacy is negatively associated with population density but is *not* directly associated with census tract measures of concentrated disadvantage and residential stability.

Model 3 also indicates that homeownership is statistically associated with collective efficacy (see Table 8.2). On this outcome, collective efficacy, homeowners score 0.17 higher than comparable renters. Thus, results for all three models show statistically significant effects for homeownership. Controlling for all else, owning a home has a direct, positive effect on sense of community, willingness to fix problems, and collective efficacy. Additionally, this homeownership effect is evident while controlling for neighborhood residential stability and *after* the propensity score analysis that adjusts for selectivity by matching renters to owners.

Consequently, these findings suggest that there could be something about homeownership itself that leads people to feel a higher of sense of community with their neighborhoods *and* to consider that their neighbors have a greater willingness to fix problems. Both of these aspects translate into higher levels of collective efficacy among homeowners. Next, we consider how homeownership and collective efficacy might relate to perceptions of crime.

Table 8.3 displays results of regression models for the second key outcome, crime perceptions, on the same variables we used to predict sense of community, willingness to fix problems, and collective efficacy. Recall that perceived crime is an indicator for those 16.5% of respondents who said that crime is the biggest problem in their neighborhood.

Results from Table 8.3 indicate that this measure of perceived crime is associated with several predictors. The census tract measure of neighborhood disadvantage correlates positively with crime perceptions; that is, crime is more likely to be seen as a major problem in disadvantaged neighborhoods. This finding illustrates the

TABLE 8.3

Crime Perceptions Regressed on Homeownership via Collective Efficacy
Crime Is the Biggest Problem In the Neighborhood
Model 3, Panel B

Direct Pathways	
Homeowner (compared to renter)	−0.03
Self-efficacy	0.24*
Age (51 years or older)	0.06
Income (Relative to area median income)	−0.08
Neighborhood disadvantage	0.43*
Neighborhood population density	−0.01
Neighborhood residential stability	−0.09
Collective Efficacy	−0.95*
Indirect Pathways	
Neighborhood residential stability via collective efficacy	−0.05
Homeownership via collective efficacy	−0.16*

N = 750. Crime is identified as the biggest problem in the neighborhood by 124 (16.5%) respondents. Of these, 52 (42%) were homeowners and 72 (58%) were renters. Model 3 has two outcomes, collective efficacy (Panel A) and crime perceptions (Panel B), and continues from Table 8.2, which is used to compute estimates for the two indirect pathways.
* means statistically significant.

impact of poverty, unemployment, and other structural factors on perceived crime. Collective efficacy, the new predictor for this model, also performs as expected. There is a negative association of collective efficacy with crime perceptions. With each one-point increase on the four-point collective efficacy anchor, there is a 0.95 reduction in the likelihood of perceiving crime as a neighborhood problem.

These associations with perceived crime adjust for household demographic characteristics such as income and self-efficacy. Notably, Table 8.3 displays a nonsignificant effect for homeownership. Thus, Table 8.3 shows that there is no *direct* relationship between owning a home and identifying crime as the biggest problem in the neighborhood. There is, however, evidence of an indirect effect for homeownership. Whereas the prior estimates can be described as direct pathways between predictor and outcome, we also test two new indirect pathways. By *indirect*, we mean that an intervening variable comes between the predictor and outcome. An indirect pathway combines two direct paths. Thus, we identify the potential for indirect pathways by connecting select predictors with the two key outcomes for Model 3: collective efficacy (see Table 8.2) and perceived crime (see Table 8.3).[4]

In this way, we investigate how crime perceptions might relate to homeownership and neighborhood residential stability using both direct and indirect pathways. The lower rows of Table 8.3 show the results for two indirect pathways for these variables through collective efficacy. Neighborhood residential stability via collective efficacy is not a statistically significant predictor of crime perceptions; however, homeownership via collective efficacy is statistically significant. This indirect pathway is the positive effect of homeownership on collective efficacy (0.17) times the negative effect of collective efficacy on perceived crime (−0.95). Thus, the total effect of homeownership on perceptions of crime as the biggest neighborhood problem is negative (−0.16). This indicates that the indirect effect of homeownership—through collective efficacy—is associated with a lower likelihood of perceiving crime as the biggest neighborhood problem. In other words, homeownership is negatively associated with crime perceptions, but indirectly, through the social process of collective efficacy.

Conclusion

The purpose of this chapter was to examine how homeownership relates to two key outcomes—collective efficacy and the perception of crime in the neighborhood. We first examined the relationship of homeownership to the building blocks of collective efficacy: sense of community and a willingness to fix problems. We found a statistically significant positive effect for homeownership with these building blocks as well as the broader dimension of collective efficacy.

We then explored links to respondents' perceptions of crime in the neighborhood. As expected, we find no direct effect for homeownership—that is, homeowners are neither more nor less likely than similar renters to directly perceive crime as the biggest problem in the neighborhood. However, we do uncover a statistically significant indirect effect for homeownership. Recall that collective efficacy is negatively associated with crime perceptions and that homeownership is positively associated with collective efficacy. Our analysis connects these pathways and provides a test of mediation showing that homeownership is, in fact, negatively associated with crime perceptions—but indirectly, through the social process of collective efficacy.

These findings are consistent with existing theory as originally conceived by Sampson and colleagues (1997). We contribute by explicitly addressing the respondent's decision to own or rent the home. We show that a homeownership effect persists after adjusting for the selectivity of owning or renting, as well as other competing explanations, including household mobility and neighborhood residential stability.

By demonstrating that a homeownership effect exists among our sample of lower-income homeowners, all of whom received traditional, fixed-rate mortgages, we draw attention to sustainable homeownership opportunities as a tool for policymakers. When combined with quality mortgages, homeownership has the capacity to help revitalize neighborhoods through its direct association with higher levels of collective efficacy and indirect association with reduced perceptions of crime. In these ways, homeownership itself has the potential to enhance the safety and security of neighborhoods.

If the future of housing finance continues to be one of constrained mortgage lending and relatively large down-payment requirements, then the coming decades are likely to be characterized by fewer homeownership opportunities in which lower-income households delay their first home purchase or opt to rent permanently. As lower-income households remain renters for longer periods, will they feel a stronger sense of community within their neighborhoods? Will long-term renters develop a greater willingness to fix neighborhood problems that our empirical findings associate with homeowners? These developments are possible but may require changes to the structure of tenant leases or changes in the tradition of homeownership opportunities and mortgage lending, such as shared equity mortgages or lease-purchase programs (Thaden, Greer, & Saegert 2013). For potential homeowners, expanded mortgage credit availability and lower down-payment requirements can help lower-income households receive the quality, fixed-rate mortgages that have traditionally led to successful homeownership experiences.

Our study provides evidence that homeownership is positively associated with collective efficacy and—indirectly—is negatively associated with perceiving crime as a neighborhood problem. Such perceptions matter because they have been linked to residents' physical and mental health (Ross 2000; Ross & Mirowsky 2001). Note that the impact of homeownership is not direct but rather operates through collective efficacy, which we measure by specifying a new role for sense of community as social cohesion. Overall, our study identifies the robust yet indirect role of homeownership, through collective efficacy, in curtailing the perceptions of neighborhood crime.

Notes

1. The terminology we use here differs slightly from that used by Sampson and colleagues (1997). We use the term *sense of community* to refer to what they called "social cohesion," and we use the term *willingness to fix problems* to refer to what they called "informal social control." The underlying constructs and key measures are the same.

2. We combine items using a data reduction technique called confirmatory factor analysis.

This technique assesses similarities and differences between items and combines them into an index. In traditional index construction, items are given equal weight and then summed. Survey items are assumed to be measured without error. In contrast, our approach models the error terms for each survey item and then weights each item according to how strongly it contributes to the underlying concept. In this way, the items contribute in varying degrees to the two elements, sense of community and willingness to fix problems. Because we agree with prior researchers who conceive of these as distinct elements, we combine the items for each element separately.

3. For space and presentation considerations, we do not display these nonsignificant effects.

4. These estimates are produced simultaneously, from the same model. We place the estimates for these two outcomes on separate tables to help organize the presentation of results. These are shown respectively as Table 8.2 (Model 3, Panel A) and Table 8.3 (Model 3, Panel B).

9 Homeownership: Mechanisms and Dependencies

THROUGHOUT THIS BOOK, we have explored a wide range of social outcomes associated with homeownership. We have found that homeownership is linked to positive outcomes; for example, homeowners are more likely to vote in local elections, participate in neighborhood groups, and be connected to neighbors who can help them navigate challenges and fix problems. Homeowners are also less likely to experience physical and mental health problems and are more likely to report better health overall. These patterns are consistent with what other researchers have found (Dietz & Haurin 2003; Herbert & Belsky 2008; Rohe & Lindblad 2014; Rohe, Van Zandt, & McCarthy 2002).

What is different about the findings presented in this book is that we have adjusted for the key challenge of selection bias. That is, the studies presented in prior chapters reveal positive associations with owning a home even after addressing the concern that people do not randomly become homeowners or renters. The outcomes we have investigated involve private consequences, such as better health, and social consequences, such as greater civic engagement. In all cases, these outcomes can be considered nonfinancial benefits. Having adjusted for selectivity bias throughout this book, we still uncover a consistently positive effect linking homeownership to nonfinancial benefits.

What remains unclear is *why* homeownership is associated with nonfinancial benefits. This question matters for two key reasons. First, an improved understanding of how homeownership influences outcomes can help inform the development of sustainable housing policies. Second, and perhaps more importantly, knowing why homeownership matters can help policymakers extend these benefits to renters.

We are not the first to consider this question of why homeownership matters. Researchers typically evaluate the correlates of owning a home and then infer why homeownership is related to private and social benefits. The most common example of this approach involves the assumption of financial interests—that is, many researchers, ourselves included, observe homeowners performing more socially desirable behaviors than renters, and then they attribute this pattern to the financial interests inherent to owning a home. The problem with this approach is that the financial interest explanation is presumed, not tested. Similarly, most other explanations for homeownership effects have been inferred rather than assessed (Rohe et al. 2002). Because few studies have empirically investigated the underlying factors involved, there is little evidence regarding which processes drive the homeownership effects observed.

In this chapter, we address this research gap in three ways. First, we present a conceptual framework for how and why homeownership might influence nonfinancial benefits. Second, we assess our conceptual framework empirically; in particular, we focus on the health and civic engagement outcomes that we have studied in this book. Our findings separate the mechanisms that transfer the benefits of homeownership from the dependencies, or related factors, that alter the degree to which the benefits are transferred. We find that the mechanisms— the amount of time lived in the home and the perceived control of the survey respondent—transfer benefits such as civic engagement and positive health outcomes. Additionally, we find that the transfer of these benefits relies on factors, or dependencies, such as housing type and level of home equity. Third and lastly, we use our empirical findings to suggest ways in which the nonfinancial benefits associated with homeownership might be applied more broadly.

Background

In this section, we review the literature around the reasons why owning a home might lead to nonfinancial benefits. We identify four possible mechanisms: residential stability, perceived control, social identity, and financial interests. We then consider several confounds and dependencies that could change or moderate the potential effects of homeownership: the quality of the dwelling, whether the

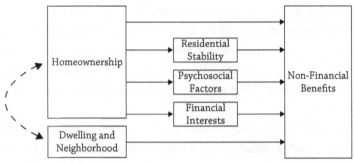

FIGURE 9.1 The homeownership effect.

housing structure is detached from other buildings, and the level of equity in the home. Before discussing our analysis and presenting our results, we present our conceptual framework.

Figure 9.1 illustrates our theory of the homeownership effect. The upper arrow shows the direct effect typically assessed by scholars. The lower arrow displays the confounding influences of the participant's dwelling and neighborhood. Because these upper and lower arrows flow uninterrupted between predictor and outcome, we call them *direct* effects. The middle arrows of Figure 9.1 represent the pathways through which the benefits of homeownership may be conveyed. The center boxes show that residential stability, psychosocial factors, and financial interests help explain why homeownership is associated with nonfinancial benefits. We refer to these center boxes as the mechanisms of homeownership. Note that the mechanisms shown in the center boxes involve two arrows—one arrow enters from homeownership and one arrow exits toward the nonfinancial benefit. Combined, these two arrows form a pathway called an *indirect effect*.

A curved line connects the two boxes to the left, (1) homeownership and (2) dwelling and neighborhood. This curve indicates that, in the United States, homeownership opportunities tend to be connected to particular types of dwellings and neighborhoods. To simplify the analysis, we do not model this curved path, thus the dotted rather than solid line.[1]

Mechanisms

Having provided our conceptual framework of the homeownership effect, we now turn to the mechanisms involved. We review the literature around the reasons that owning a home might lead to nonfinancial benefits. We consider four potential mechanisms: residential stability, perceived control, social identity, and financial interests.

Residential Stability

Homeowners are known to move less frequently than renters. The primary reason that scholars have given for this lower mobility of homeowners is the time and expense of selling a home. Because these transaction costs of selling are substantial, homeowners are less mobile than renters (Dietz & Haurin 2003; DiPasquale & Glaeser 1999; Herbert & Belsky 2008; Newman & Holupka 2013; Rohe & Stewart 1996).

It may follow that people who expect to live in their neighborhood for longer periods are more inclined to become involved in community affairs. Because selling and moving are expensive transactions, homeowners could be more motivated than renters to address problems in their neighborhood. In turn, the

> I like having my own house and not having to move.

greater residential stability induced by homeownership may lower the expenses and stressors associated with moving, thus improving educational attainment for children and health outcomes for all household members. In this way, residential stability—measured as the length of time participants have lived in their dwellings—could explain many of the effects of homeownership. It is also possible that residential stability could be extended to renters with longer-term leases.

Perceived Control

Homeowners decide whether and how to maintain their home. They also customize their dwellings, whereas the landlord controls many features of the dwelling for most renters. Most importantly, renters have substantially less control than homeowners do over how long they live in their residence. In these ways, owning a home increases an individual's actual control over his or her dwelling, which may in turn lead to greater perceived control over life events (Megbolugbe & Linneman 1993; Rohe & Basolo 1997; Rohe & Stegman 1994a). Greater perceived control

> It's mine ... I don't have to worry if my grandchildren come over. I can do what I want. I have the freedom to do what I please with my house ... I can paint my kitchen red.

may improve satisfaction and health and encourage social involvement in neighborhoods. This is another mechanism that could potentially be extended to some renters, perhaps through changes to the structuring of tenant leases.

Social Identity

Traditionally, homeownership has signified socially desirable attributes such as industriousness, citizenship, and higher social status (Megbolugbe & Linneman

> I rented until I got my home. Then I became stable and brought my confidence up. Owning a home is the American Dream and I am glad I did it. I love it. Expenses go up and down, but I love it.

> Homeownership gives me a sense of pride.

1993; Rossi & Weber 1996). Homeownership has been found to be part of the "package deal," along with marriage, career, and children, that signified success to society (Townsend 2002). Perhaps most notably, homeownership has long been regarded as a cornerstone of the American Dream (McCabe 2016; Quercia, Freeman, & Ratcliffe 2011). This social and cultural value attached to homeownership may lead home-owners to report greater life satisfaction and higher self-esteem (Balfour & Smith 1996; Dietz & Haurin 2003; Rohe & Stegman 1994a; Rossi & Weber 1996). As a positive social identity, home-ownership may carry expectations alongside it, such as greater involvement in community affairs. This potential mechanism would be more difficult to extend to renters, because it would involve changing cultural norms.

Financial Interests

Homeowners have property interests that are distinct from those of renters. The home is the largest purchase most people ever make, and its value depends on not only the property itself, but also the value of nearby properties. These property values reflect to a large degree the availability of local amenities, such as schools, parks, roadways, restaurants, and grocery stores. Thus, homeowners have an incentive to become more involved in community affairs in order to ensure that their financial investment in the home does not lose value.

> My homeownership experience has been up and down, the cost of living has increased and I have not made more money, so I struggle month to month, and because of foreclosures my homeowner's association fees went up.

Homeowners and renters alike have a "use interest" in their property—they both derive value from using neighbor-hood amenities—but only homeowners have a financial interest in maintaining their property and neighborhood (Rohe & Stewart 1996). Many researchers suggest that these unique financial motives may explain homeowners' higher rates of social involvement (Dietz & Haurin 2003; Rohe & Mouw 1991; Rohe & Stegman 1994a; Rohe & Stewart 1996; Rohe et al. 2000). If financial interests are a mechanism for conveying the benefits of homeownership, then changes to the tax code may be needed to extend these benefits to renters.

Dependencies

The mechanisms listed in the prior section are thought to stem from homeownership itself. Yet some of the homeownership effect could also be explained by factors that are associated with—yet not directly caused by—the decision to own or rent. While some factors can alter or confound the homeownership effect, they are not causally determined by owning a home. Therefore, we call these *dependencies*. We discuss three particular dependencies here: dwelling type, dwelling quality, and home equity.

Dwelling Type

The type and quality of the residential dwelling could be related to the benefits that have been associated with homeownership. Dwelling type—also referred to as housing structure—is associated with the decision to own or rent, as renters are more likely to live in attached units such as apartments, while homeowners tend to live in detached buildings. But dwelling type is not causally determined by owning or renting; many tenants rent single-family detached houses. Similarly, condominiums and townhomes are attached to other housing units, yet these are primary residences that usually involve mortgages and do constitute homeownership.

> I enjoy living in a house instead of an apartment because of freedom and space.

These differences in the types of building structures that people inhabit could affect the residential experience. In particular, the social experience with neighbors could be influenced by whether the resident lives in a detached building or a building that is attached to other units. This is because socializing with neighbors may be more likely and frequent in attached dwellings where people share walls and live more closely. Thus, whether the housing structure is a single-family home, townhouse, apartment, condominium, or mobile home may relate to the attitudes and behaviors of residents (Barker 2013; Dietz & Haurin 2003; Herbert & Belsky 2008; Rohe et al. 2000).

> Because I live in a townhouse, we live close together, so sometimes I hear my neighbors from my house. Other than that, I love my house.

Dwelling Quality

Another feature that has the potential to alter the residential experience is the quality of the dwelling. Homes that are owned by the primary resident can, of course, be poorly maintained, with a leaky roof, defective plumbing, broken

> The landlord doesn't fix up the repairs when we report them. We had a broken toilet for two years ... I kept complaining but maintenance doesn't like to come out.

> I like apartment life because if anything breaks down, I pick up the phone and call the landlord ... no shoveling snow or cutting grass!

appliances, electrical problems, or vermin. Such home maintenance problems likely reduce housing satisfaction, but they may also be linked to personal health and community involvement. Conversely, a dwelling can be of very high quality, yet not be owned by the resident. In fact, landlords can charge higher rents for apartments that are well designed and outfitted. As these examples illustrate, the quality of the resident's dwelling is *not* linked in a causal way to whether or not the resident owns the dwelling. In these ways, the type and quality of the residential dwelling might alter the benefits that are typically associated with homeownership. Yet most studies of homeownership neglect these features of the dwelling (Barker 2013; Dietz & Haurin 2003; Herbert & Belsky 2008; Rohe et al. 2000).

Home Equity

Lastly, we consider home equity to be an important factor upon which the possible benefits of homeownership may depend. The value of a home can be affected by events outside the homeowner's control. A good example of this occurred during the Great Recession of 2008–2010. Home values dropped in response to a mortgage lending crisis and widespread foreclosures. Even homeowners who were never delinquent on their mortgages experienced large declines in house value. Because the value of the homes dropped, home equity—the difference between the value of the home and what is owed on the mortgage—also declined. Declines in home value can be substantial enough that the mortgage becomes "underwater," a situation in which the homeowner owes more to the bank than the property is worth. In such cases, the homeowner cannot sell the property for profit. Selling property when it is underwater can trigger financial losses if, upon sale, money is still owed to the bank.

> I like the house I live in, but because of foreclosures, the value went down.

When homeowners have little or no equity in their home, financial stressors can be compounded. For example, as unemployment surged in the Great Recession, the incomes of many homeowners decreased. Homeowners who had difficulty paying bills while holding property with little or no home equity faced greater financial stressors. For these reasons, low levels of home equity may be associated with greater stress and diminished health. Conversely, higher levels of home equity signal greater household wealth, which may be linked to higher satisfaction, better health outcomes, or greater community involvement. Only a few empirical studies have explored these possibilities.

Some scholars have considered how home values relate to positive social outcomes such as volunteering and school attendance. In one study, Rotolo, Wilson, and Hughes (2010) examined relations between volunteering and home values, which partly determine home equity. The researchers tested self-reported home values as high, low, or none (for renters) by using the median of home value to create upper and lower categories. The findings suggest that there is no association between home values and volunteering. A study by Green, Painter, and White (2012) analyzed home equity at the time of home purchase, as measured by the size of the mortgage down payment. Their study adjusted for selection into homeownership and time lived in the dwelling. Their findings showed that children of homeowners are less likely to drop out of high school. The size of the mortgage down payment did not influence high school dropout rates, except when homes were purchased with no down payment at all.

Both of these studies used respondent's self-assessments for home values and mortgage down payment, which equals home equity at home purchase. Neither study found strong support for the idea that home equity alters nonfinancial outcomes. While it makes conceptual sense that the nonfinancial benefits of homeownership could depend upon positive equity in the home, there have been few empirical studies in this area. In this chapter, we consider the possibility that home equity, along with dwelling type and quality, could alter the homeownership effect.

Analysis

Our analysis tests some of the field's key theoretical contentions: (1) that homeownership conveys nonfinancial benefits (while adjusting for selectivity in the decision to own or rent); (2) that the factors underlying the homeownership effect can be explicitly tested; and (3) that the benefits of homeownership are dependent upon the features of dwellings that are associated with, but not directly caused by, owning. Before presenting our results, we identify indicators for the two kinds of outcomes we examine: civic engagement and health. We then detail the measures that we use to assess the mechanisms and dependencies by which homeownership conveys nonfinancial benefits (some of these measures were also used in earlier chapters of this volume). Finally, we describe the analytic techniques that we use to assess whether and how these factors underlie the homeownership effect.

Measuring Outcomes

We assess several civic engagement and health outcomes, measuring each with single-item survey questions. We present the question wording and %ages below.

Civic Engagement

To assess civic engagement, we use questions in the areas of both instrumental and expressive civic engagement and local voting participation. Although general political involvement and voting were found to be unrelated to homeownership in a field experiment (Engelhardt et al. 2010), here we assess voting in local rather than national elections. This focus on local elections makes theoretical sense as well given that homeowners should be more likely to participate locally due to their greater financial interest in the neighborhood. The four civic engagement outcomes and their respective questions follow:

- Participation: "Do you currently participate in any neighborhood-based group, like a homeowners or tenants association, neighborhood improvement group, block crime watch, or other community service group?" Yes (18.7%), No (81.3%)
- Voting: "Did you vote in the last local election?" Yes (43.8%), No (56.2%)
- Conversations: "In the past month, how many times have you had a conversation with a neighbor? Would you say never (7.1%), once or twice (20.3%), once a week or less (26.5%), or more than once a week (46.1%)?"
- Friends: "How many of your neighbors are your friends? Would you say none of them (21.9%), one or two of them (33.1%), or more than two of them (45%)?"

Health

We use self-reported measures to assess personal health, taking overall health as well as physical and mental health limitations into consideration. These items come from the short-form health survey that was validated by Ware, Kosinski, and Keller (1996) and Jenkinson and colleagues (1997). The questions and responses for the three health outcomes follow:

- General Health: "In general, would you say your health is excellent (19.1%), very good (26.6%), good (35.4%), fair (14.7%), or poor (4.3%)?"

TABLE 9.1

Descriptive Statistics

Construct	Measure	Mean	Median	Std. Dev.
Residential stability	Years lived in dwelling	3.74	5.00	1.71
Perceived control	Sense of control	3.63	3.75	0.75
	Self-efficacy	2.25	2.00	1.06
Social identity	Years parents owned	12.13	17.00	7.31
	Peers who own homes	5.49	6.00	1.47
Financial interest	User cost of housing	5,847	718	13,950
Dwelling	Dwelling quality	7.89	8.00	1.75
	Single-family house	0.61	n/a	n/a

Sample size is 1,138.

- Physical Health Limitation: "During the past four weeks, were you limited in the kind of work or other regular activities you do as a result of your physical health?" Yes (18.9%), No (81.1%)
- Mental Health Problem: "During the past four weeks, have you accomplished less than you would like to as a result of any emotional problems such as feeling depressed or anxious?" Yes (16.8%), No (83.2%)

Measuring Mechanisms

In this section, we describe how we measure the homeownership mechanisms of residential stability, psychosocial factors, and financial interests. Descriptive statistics are shown in Table 9.1.

Residential Stability

We measure residential stability using the amount of time the respondent has lived in his or her dwelling, and more specifically as the respondent's number of years lived in the dwelling. We recode the upper end to create a ceiling of five or more years. This measure largely overlaps with the amount of time lived in the neighborhood, which we therefore drop to avoid redundancy.

Psychosocial Measures

The psychosocial indicators measure the respondent's perceived control and social identity as a homeowner. For the dimension of perceived control, we consider two items, *sense of control* and *self-efficacy*. The sense of control variable is an index that measures the extent to which people perceive that they have control over their lives. The index comes from the Perceived Stress Scale (Cohen et al. 1983). Higher scores indicate more perceived control. Using five-point Likert-style response options that ranged from "never" to "very often," participants were asked to assess their past 12 months using the following four items: "How often have you felt that you were unable to control the important things in your life?"; "How often have you felt confident about your ability to handle your personal problems?"; "How often have you felt that things were going your way?"; and "How often have you felt difficulties were piling up so high that you could not overcome them?" We combined these measures and then divided by the number of items in the index to derive average scores that are anchored to the survey response options. This sense of control variable averages 3.63 on a scale that ranges from one to five.

Self-efficacy measures whether respondents think that people like themselves can make a difference on neighborhood problems. Respondents were asked: "Overall, how much of a difference do you think people like you can make on [reducing crime, improving schools, unemployment, neighborhood change, traffic, etc.]," where the four response options range from "no difference at all" to "a big difference," and the bracketed text is filled with the response to the previous question, "What do you consider to be the biggest problem in your neighborhood?" This self-efficacy measure is identical to that used in the preceding chapter on collective efficacy.

For the second psychosocial dimension, the social identity of homeownership, we consider two additional measures: *years parents owned* and *peers who own homes*. The first measure is the number of years in which the respondent's parents owned a home during the respondent's childhood. Ranging from 0 to 18 years, we expect that when parents owned homes for longer periods of time during the respondent's childhood, the respondent had greater opportunities to become socialized to the manner in which homeowners are expected to behave. The second measure, peers who own homes, is derived from two questions: "How many of your friends own homes?" and "How many of your family members own homes?" (response options were all, most, some, or none). We code responses so that higher values indicate more people and then combine responses to both questions.

Financial Interests

Lastly, we consider that financial factors may play a part in the transfer of the benefits of homeownership. We measure the *user cost of housing* to assess the financial cost of owning versus renting a home. This measure includes not only the monthly mortgage or rent payment but also utilities and taxes. More specifically,

> Owning a home is not as stressful as having to rent, and having a home is something I will have for the future . . . I am not giving away money.

the cost of homeownership includes mortgage payments, maintenance expenses, taxes, and insurance premiums. The cost of renting is the monthly rent that would have been paid on a comparable property. Construction of this user cost of housing variable is complex and drawn from multiple measures. This measure was used in the study by Riley and colleagues (2013), which showed that owning a home cost less than renting while controlling for house prices, the timing of home purchase, and the length of homeownership.

Measuring Dependencies

Measurements for potential dependencies—dwelling type, dwelling quality, and home equity—are detailed below. The key distinction between these dependencies and the mechanisms described in the prior section is the relationship to homeownership: The mechanisms are causally determined by owning a home, while the dependencies are related to—but not determined by—homeownership. We measure three dependencies that may alter the homeownership effect: dwelling type, dwelling quality, and home equity.

Dwelling Type and Quality

Respondents indicated whether they lived in an apartment, condominium, townhome, single-family home, or other type of residence. We used the following question to gauge dwelling quality: "On a scale of 1 to 10, where 1 is the worst and 10 is the best, how would you rate your [dwelling type] as a place to live?"

Home Equity

We use a subjective measure of home equity instead of actual house price valuations because, in our view, this self-reported home equity measure provides a more direct link to the respondent's health and civic engagement. Our homeowners were asked, "How much equity do you currently have in your home?"[2] We use the 33rd and 67th percentiles to create high, medium, and low categories of subjective home equity.

Analytic Strategy

To assess our conception of mechanisms and dependencies, we attempt to empirically test the paths we laid out in Figure 9.1. Our approach is similar to that used in the prior chapter on collective efficacy. Recall from the description of Figure 9.1 that the center boxes interrupt the flow between predictor and outcome to jointly form an indirect effect of homeownership. Thus, we hypothesize that the mechanisms shown in the center box of Figure 9.1 will interrupt the causal flow that prior research has found between homeownership and nonfinancial benefits. As discussed, we hypothesize indirect effects for homeownership through several mechanisms: residential stability (time in dwelling), psychosocial factors (perceived control, social identity), and financial interests (user cost of housing). If the pathways, or specific indirect effects, of these mechanisms are statistically significant, then the findings would suggest that the intervening variable is a mechanism of homeownership.

Thus, our goal in this analysis is to determine whether factors related to the experience of homeownership explain away some of the direct effect of homeownership. To the extent they do, the findings may suggest why homeownership is associated with nonfinancial benefits. Furthermore, the findings may imply that some of the benefits of homeownership could be extended to renters. We do not expect these intervening variables to fully explain the homeownership effect. Therefore, we also specify a direct effect for homeownership, which is shown as the upper line of Figure 9.1. The direct and indirect effects sum to a *total homeownership effect*.

Results

The civic engagement and health outcomes for this chapter have been reviewed in earlier parts of this book. We use the same data and first match renters to homeowners before the path analysis. Our findings build from simpler to more complex models. We are most interested in identifying factors that underlie (mechanisms) or alter (dependencies) the homeownership effect. Initially, we identify direct effects—these reveal findings for homeownership and dwelling type. We then turn to models that identify indirect effects for homeownership through the mechanisms of residential stability and perceived control. Finally, we show how the effect of homeownership through these mechanisms can depend on higher levels of home equity. At the end of this section, we provide a summary of findings.

Homeownership and Dwelling Type: Direct Effects

First, we display results for a model showing statistically significant paths for direct effects. These direct effects are indicated by the upper and lower arrows of Figure 9.1. The outcome that we model is whether or not the respondent belonged to a neighborhood group—also called *instrumental civic engagement* in Chapter 6. Model 1 in Table 9.2 indicates that the direct effect of homeownership

TABLE 9.2

Neighborhood Group Participation Regressed on Homeownership and Dwelling

Predictor	Effect	Model 1 Homeownership		Model 2 Plus Dwelling	
		Estimate	Odds Ratio	Estimate	Odds Ratio
Homeownership	Direct	0.75*	2.12	1.16*	3.14
Dwelling quality	Direct			0.10	1.10
Single-family house	Direct			−1.04*	0.35

Sample size is 1,127. Participation in a neighborhood-based group = No (81.3%), Yes (18.7%). *Estimation:* Binary logistic regression. Model specification controls for household income.
*Result is statistically significant (p < 0.05).

on neighborhood group participation is statistically significant and positive. With an odds ratio of 2.12, the direct effect shows that homeowners are 112% more likely than similar renters to participate in neighborhood groups. The second model provides insight about this homeownership effect.

Model 2 adds two potential dependencies, that is, variables related to the respondent's dwelling that may alter a homeownership effect but are not causally determined by owning. Results for the first variable indicate that the quality of the dwelling is not a statistically significant predictor of neighborhood group participation.[3] However, results show that there is a direct effect on neighborhood group participation for the *type* of dwelling. Detached, single-family houses have a negative estimate, with an odds ratio of 0.35. This result indicates that respondents who live in detached housing are substantially *less* likely to participate in neighborhood groups. Once we adjust for this negative effect of detached, single-family houses, the direct homeownership effect increases from 2.12 in Model 1 to 3.14 in Model 2. Thus, the addition of the dwelling structure—detached housing—does not diminish the effects of homeownership on neighborhood group participation. To the contrary, the homeownership effect *increases* when we control for dwelling type. Interestingly, this result suggests that the nonfinancial benefits of owning a home may be lower in detached housing, such as single-family houses, and greater for attached housing, such as townhomes and condominiums.

Mechanisms of Homeownership: Indirect Effects

The results presented in the prior section are direct effects on neighborhood group participation in which the pathway flows uninterrupted between predictor and outcome. These direct effects are illustrated with the upper and lower arrows of Figure 9.1. Next, we turn to the pathways for the center boxes of Figure 9.1.

TABLE 9.3

Local Voting Regressed on Homeownership

Construct	Predictor	Effect	Estimate	Odds Ratio
Owning	Homeownership	Total	0.61*	1.83
		Direct	0.31	1.36
Residential stability	Years in dwelling	Indirect	0.23*	1.25
Perceived control	Sense of control	Indirect	0.02	1.02
	Self-efficacy	Indirect	0.04	1.04
Social identity	Years parents owned	Indirect	0.02	1.02
	Peers who own homes	Indirect	ns	
Financial interest	User cost of housing	Indirect	ns	

Sample size is 1,127.

Estimation: Binary logistic regression of "voted in the last local election" = No (56.2%), Yes (43.8%).

Model specification controls for household income. The "ns" refers to "not significant" estimates for peers who own homes and user cost of housing. These variables introduce missing data that reduce sample sizes by more than 35%. Neither variable is statistically significant for any outcomes. Due to smaller samples sizes, displaying these estimates would require additional models; instead, we simplify by putting "ns" here and omitting these rows from ensuing tables.

*Result is statistically significant (p < 0.05).

Because the center boxes interrupt the flow between predictor and outcome, they are potential mechanisms that connect pathways that jointly form potential indirect effects for homeownership. These indirect effects combine with direct effects to form a total homeownership effect.

Table 9.3 presents these total, direct, and indirect effects of homeownership for a model that specifies whether or not the respondent voted in the last local election. The total effect of homeownership on local voting is statistically significant and positive, but the direct effect is not. This result suggests that the impact of homeownership on local voting is mediated by one or more of the indirect effects.

Financial Interests—The User Cost of Housing

The bottom row of Table 9.3 shows results for the user cost of housing variable as a mediator of homeownership. This variable is not statistically significant; thus, the respondent's cost of housing does not explain the association of homeownership with local voting. In fact, the user cost of housing is not statistically significant for any civic engagement or health outcomes, and so we trim it from further models.[4]

Social Identity

We estimate the effects of the social identity of homeownership using two variables: years parents owned and peers who own homes. Table 9.3 shows that neither of these estimates is statistically significant. We estimate the effects of these variables on all outcomes and find that they do not significantly mediate homeownership. This nonsignificant finding means that our measures of social identity do not help explain why homeownership is associated with civic engagement and health.[5]

Residential Stability

Table 9.3 shows the effect of four indirect effects of homeownership: years in dwelling (0.23), sense of control (0.02), self-efficacy (0.04), and years parents owned a home (0.02). Of these indirect estimates, only years in dwelling significantly mediates the impact of homeownership on local voting. The odds ratio (1.25) indicates that, for each additional year lived in the dwelling, the odds of voting in the last local election are 25% higher for homeowners than for similar renters.

Table 9.4 presents the results for two outcomes: conversations with neighbors in the past month (Model 4)—also called *expressive civic engagement* in Chapter 6—and neighbors who are friends (Model 5). The findings for both of these outcomes are similar to those for local voting. That is, the direct effect of homeownership

TABLE 9.4

Socializing with Neighbors Regressed on Homeownership

Predictor	Effect	Model 4 Conversations		Model 5 Friends	
		Estimate	Odds Ratio	Estimate	Odds Ratio
Homeownership	Total	0.15	1.16	0.58*	1.79
	Direct	−0.12	0.89	0.21	1.23
Years in dwelling	Indirect	0.22*	1.25	0.32*	1.38
Sense of control	Indirect	0.02	1.02	0.01	1.01
Self-efficacy	Indirect	0.01	1.01	0.02	1.02
Years parents owned	Indirect	0.02	1.02	0.03	1.03

Sample size is 1,127.

Estimations: Ordinal logistic regression of "conversations with a neighbor in past month" = Never (7.1%), once or twice (20.3%), once a week or less (26.5%), more than once a week (46.1%). Ordinal logistic regression of "neighbors who are friends" = None (21.9%), one or two (33.1%), more than two (45%). Model specification controls for household income.

*Result is statistically significant ($p < 0.05$).

is not significant while the indirect effect of homeownership flows uniquely through the number of years the participant has lived in the house. Together, these findings show that household residential stability—as measured by years in dwelling—completely and uniquely mediates the association of homeownership with local voting, frequency of conversations with neighbors, and the number of neighbors the participant considers as friends.

Perceived Control

Two measures of perceived control are estimated as mediators of homeownership: sense of control and self-efficacy. Neither of these measures is a statistically significant mediator in any of the community engagement outcomes.[6] However, sense of control mediates homeownership in several of the following models related to health.

Table 9.5 presents the results of two specifications related to health problems. Model 6 in Table 9.5 shows the results of an analysis about whether the participant reported being limited in regular activities during the past four weeks as a result of physical health. Sense of control partly mediates the effect of homeownership in reducing by 8% the likelihood that participants will be limited in regular activities due to their physical health.

TABLE 9.5

Health Problems Regressed on Homeownership

| | | Model 6 | | Model 7 | |
| | | Physical Limitation | | Emotional Problem | |
Predictor	Effect	Estimate	Odds Ratio	Estimate	Odds Ratio
Homeownership	Total	−0.40*	0.67	−0.27	0.76
	Direct	−0.48*	0.62	−0.11	0.90
Years in dwelling	Indirect	0.16	1.17	0.00	1.00
Sense of control	Indirect	−0.08*	0.93	−0.16*	0.85
Self-efficacy	Indirect	−0.01	0.99	−0.01	0.99
Years parents owned	Indirect	0.02	1.02	0.00	1.00

Sample size is 1,138.

Estimations: Binary logistic regression of "limited in the kind of work or other regular activities during past four weeks as a result of physical health" = No (81.1%), Yes (18.9%). Binary logistic regression of "accomplished less than would like to during past four weeks as a result of an emotional problem, such as feeling depressed or anxious" = No (83.2%), Yes (16.8%).

Model specification controls for household income.

*Result is statistically significant ($p < 0.05$).

Model 7 in Table 9.5 shows the results of an analysis about whether the participant accomplished less than he or she would like to during the past four weeks due to an emotional problem, such as feeling depressed or anxious. There is no direct effect for homeownership. However, sense of control is a statistically significant and unique mediator. Through sense of control, homeownership indirectly reduces by 16% the likelihood that a participant reported a mental or emotional health problem during the past four weeks. Together, these results in Models 6 and 7 indicate that sense of control mediates the negative association of homeownership with the likelihood of respondents' experiencing physical and mental health problems.

Table 9.6 shows the results of an analysis of the participant's assessment of his or her general health. The positive effect of homeownership on general health is partially mediated by the participant's sense of control. Additionally, there is an effect for dwelling type. Similar to the finding for neighborhood group participation (described earlier for Table 9.2, Model 2), we find with Model 8 a statistically significant direct effect for dwelling type. Specifically, respondents who live in detached, single-family houses report lower general health than respondents who live in attached housing.

Dependencies of Homeownership: Home Equity

If home equity influences health, then the homeownership effects observed in prior models should vary across the high, medium, and low home equity categories.[7] For

TABLE 9.6

Health Regressed on Homeownership and Dwelling

Predictor	Effect	Estimate	Odds Ratio
Homeownership	Total	0.34*	1.41
	Direct	0.36*	1.43
Years in dwelling	Indirect	−0.12	0.89
Sense of control	Indirect	0.10*	1.10
Self-efficacy	Indirect	0.01	1.01
Years parents owned	Indirect	−0.00	1.00
Dwelling			
Dwelling quality	Direct	0.05	1.05
Single-family house	Direct	−0.30*	0.74

Sample size is 1,138.

Estimation: Ordinal logistic regression of general health = poor (4.3%), fair (14.7%), good (35.4%), very good (26.6%), excellent (19.1%).

Model specification controls for household income.

*Result is statistically significant (p < 0.05).

TABLE 9.7

Health Regressed on Home Equity and Dwelling

Predictor	Effect	Estimate	Odds Ratio
High Home Equity	Total	0.39*	1.48
	Direct	0.37	1.45
Years in dwelling	Indirect	−0.12	0.89
Sense of control	Indirect	0.12*	1.13
Self-efficacy	Indirect	0.03	1.03
Years parents owned	Indirect	−0.00	1.00
Medium Home Equity	Total	0.39*	1.48
	Direct	0.37	1.45
Years in dwelling	Indirect	−0.13	0.88
Sense of control	Indirect	0.12*	1.13
Self-efficacy	Indirect	0.02	1.02
Years parents owned	Indirect	−0.00	1.00
Low Home Equity	Total	0.26	1.30
	Direct	0.34	1.40
Years in dwelling	Indirect	−0.11	0.89
Sense of control	Indirect	0.05	1.10
Self-efficacy	Indirect	−0.01	1.00
Years parents owned	Indirect	−0.00	1.00
Dwelling			
Dwelling quality	Direct	0.05	1.05
Single-family house	Direct	−0.23*	0.74

Sample size is 1,138.

Estimation: Ordinal logistic regression of general health = poor (4.3%), fair (14.7%), good (35.4%), very good (26.6%), excellent (19.1%).

Model specification controls for household income.

*Result is statistically significant ($p < 0.05$).

the general health specifications, Table 9.7 shows that homeownership mediation through sense of control varies by category of home equity. More specifically, the indirect effect of homeownership through sense of control is statistically significant for high and medium home equity and the magnitude of effects are similar. However, for low home equity, the mediating effect of sense of control is no longer significant.[8]

These results show that the mediated effect of homeownership (through sense of control) on general health is greater for those homeowners who report high or medium home equity. For homeowners who report negative or low home equity, there is no sense of control mediation. Thus, these findings indicate that the homeownership effect depends upon home equity; specifically, there is no home-ownership effect on health when homeowners report low or negative home equity.

Summary of Effects

Table 9.8 summarizes the significance and direction of effects across outcomes. Across models, four measures of indirect effects are *not* statistically significant: the user cost of housing, self-efficacy, years parents owned, and peers who own homes. Also nonsignificant across models is a potential confound, dwelling quality. Two potential dependencies do influence outcomes: home equity and type of dwelling. Furthermore, two of the hypothesized intervening variables exert consistently significant effects: Sense of control mediates all three health outcomes, and years in dwelling mediates four civic engagement outcomes. Together, these results support the key finding that residential stability and sense of control underlie the homeownership effect.

Conclusion

Homeownership has been found to be associated with many private and social benefits, yet few empirical studies have investigated why this is so. Because causal processes have been inferred rather than assessed, little is known about the ways in which the mechanisms of ownership could be leveraged for people who do not own homes. To address this gap, we suggested that residential stability, psychosocial factors, and financial interests are explanations that might relate to owning a home. Our path analysis does not fully explain the association of homeownership with health or with civic engagement, yet the findings indicate that the effect of homeownership exerts itself through two primary factors: the amount of time a person has lived in a dwelling and the sense of control that ownership imbues.

Given that our analysis does not fully explain the homeownership effect, other factors that we do not examine, such as legal context, could help explain the nonfinancial benefits of homeownership. Perhaps the most difficult aspect to untangle is the idea of homeownership as a positive social identity.

> Homeownership is a good investment. It's comforting to have the security, and it's liberating to be a homeowner. I can do whatever I want.

Many have noted that homeownership stands as cultural symbol and cornerstone of the American Dream, but we are not aware of any quantitative studies that have demonstrated whether and how this positive social identity influences outcomes. The nonsignificant effects of the two "social identity of homeownership" items

TABLE 9.8

Summary of Effects

Construct	Predictor	Effect	Health Outcomes			Civic Engagement Outcomes			
			General Health	Physical Limitation	Mental Health Problem	Participated in Neighborhood Group	Voted in Last Local Election	Converse with Local Neighbors	Neighbors are Friends
Owning	Homeownership	Total	+	−	ns	+	+	ns	+
	Homeownership	Direct	+	−	ns	+	+	ns	ns
Residential stability	Years in dwelling	Indirect	ns	ns	ns	ns	+	+	+
Perceived control	Sense of control	Indirect	+	+	+	ns	ns	ns	ns
Social identity	Self-efficacy	Indirect	ns	ns	ns	ns	ns	ns	ns
	Years parents owned	Indirect	ns	ns	ns	ns	ns	ns	ns
	Peers who own homes	Indirect	ns	ns	ns	ns	ns	ns	ns
Financial interest	User cost of housing	Indirect	ns	ns	ns	ns	ns	ns	ns
Financial interest	Home equity°	Interaction°	+	+	+	ns	ns	ns	ns
Dwelling	Dwelling quality	Direct	ns	ns	ns	ns	ns	ns	ns
	Single-family house	Direct	−	ns	ns	−	ns	ns	ns

Table summarizes effects as nonsignificant (ns), positive (+), or negative (−).

° Home equity levels (high, medium, low vs. none) were substituted for homeowner versus renter.

that we analyzed—the number of years the respondent's parents owned a home and the number of friends and family members who own homes—may simply reflect measurement limitations; these items are imperfect measures of the idea that homeownership connotes socially desirable attributes. Overall, the findings suggest that further conceptual and methodological work is needed to advance a more general theory of ownership.

We find no evidence that the user cost of housing mediates homeownership. This null finding is striking given that financial interests are a frequent rationale for homeownership effects. While more research is needed in this area, our results give reason to reconsider and scrutinize the presumption that financial interests underlie the nonfinancial benefits that have been associated with homeownership. Other mechanisms, such as residential stability and sense of control, may be more important than financial interests.

To the extent that financial interests do influence the homeownership effect, our findings suggest a dependency, or interaction, with home equity. Specifically, the indirect effect of homeownership on health—through the sense of control—depends upon subjective home equity. There is no association of homeownership with health when homeowners report low or negative equity.

Given that home equity depends largely upon nearby house prices, these findings support the notion that neighborhood house price decline, which is exacerbated by foreclosure sales, can interfere and negate an otherwise positive link between homeownership and health. Others have made such a connection, finding negative associations among mortgage delinquency, foreclosure, and health (Alley, Lloyd, Pagan, Pollack, Shardell, & Cannuscio 2011; McLaughlin, Nandi, Keyes, Uddin, Aiello, Galea, Koenen, Abramson, Metalsky, & Alloy 2012; Nettleton & Burrows 1998). However, our own research on home foreclosure sales and the related policy alternative—mortgage loan modifications—suggests that it is not foreclosure itself that leads to poorer health consequences, but rather other negative life events, such as job and income loss (Lindblad & Riley 2015). More research is needed in these areas of housing and health, and our current study contributes by suggesting that the association of homeownership with health may depend upon higher home equity.

> Everything has gone wrong ... I wouldn't buy a house again. The market has caused me to lose everything.

> I like owning the home, but I don't like to do things myself. The upkeep of the home is more than I bargained for.

By controlling for dwelling type, our analysis suggests that the structure of the dwelling changes the association of owning a home with nonfinancial benefits.

Specifically, detached housing is associated with a decrease in the effect of home-ownership on general health and participation in neighborhood groups. The reason is not clear, but one possibility is that detached dwellings discourage social involvement.[9] While future research should assess whether the influence of dwelling type interacts with that of homeownership, our findings suggest that the non-financial benefits of owning a home may be magnified in attached structures such as condominiums and townhomes. If so, then policymakers might readily transfer the nonfinancial benefits of ownership from the single-family detached dwell-ings that symbolize the tradition of homeownership and toward a greater empha-sis and stronger promotion of those attached dwellings—condominiums and townhomes—that are also owned. A potential complication is that these forms of attached housing are more susceptible to price volatility. The findings suggest that policies directed toward stabilizing house prices across all types of dwellings might also stabilize home equity and thereby improve health outcomes.

> Nobody can tell me what I can and cannot do. That's what I like about owning a home.

> My landlord is the great-est and allows me to make improvements as I like.
>
> —Renter

Two factors that were significant—residential stability and sense of control—could conceivably be broadened to include non-homeowners. With changes to tenant leases, the nonfinancial benefits of homeownership might be extended to renters. The one-year lease typifies renting in the United States. The findings suggest that higher levels of civic engagement might result if longer leases were available to renters. Similarly, health outcomes might be improved by structuring rental leases to give tenants greater control to customize their liv-ing environments. Both of these changes would help extend residential stability and a sense of con-trol to renters.

In the foreseeable future, housing in the United States is likely to be character-ized by fewer homeownership opportunities—particularly for low- and moderate-income households—due to constrained mortgage lending. Consequently, there is a need to better understand how the mechanisms that underlie the homeowner-ship effect might be leveraged to a broader social benefit. We have taken initial steps toward understanding why homeownership has been found to be associated with nonfinancial benefits and will take up this question in more detail in our concluding chapter.

We hope that our study provides a contribution, first, by proposing a conceptual framework for how the causal mechanisms that underlie homeownership might exert influence, and second, by presenting an empirical test of these competing mechanisms. Third, we hope to add to the conversation around homeownership by suggesting how the mechanisms and dependencies we have identified might be extended to renters. Our findings indicate that civic engagement and health are associated with home equity and dwelling type, yet are driven by residential stability and perceived control. With changes to existing housing policy, these factors could be leveraged to benefit people who do not own homes.

Notes

1. Although we draw this curved arrow to acknowledge current housing realities, we suggest that, *conceptually*, this curved path need not exist. With very few exceptions, there is no reason that owning itself *has* to be connected to particular types of dwellings or certain kinds of neighborhoods. For example, detached, single-family homes often come to mind when thinking about homeownership, but, in fact, our findings will show greater non-financial benefits to owning for attached structures that occupy less space: condominiums and townhomes.

2. If needed, interviewers provided clarification to define home equity.

3. In fact, *dwelling quality* is not a statistically significant predictor of any outcomes in this chapter.

4. We estimate the effect of homeownership mediation by *user cost of housing* for all other outcomes and find that it is not statistically significant in any models. This variable, *user cost of housing*, introduces missing data due to survey design and results in a 40% reduction in sample size. Given the non-significance findings for *user cost of housing* as well as the sample size that its inclusion imposes, we removed estimates for this variable from presented models. The tables show "ns" for non-significant as displaying the estimates require a different sample size and model.

5. Given non-significant findings for social identity, we remove the *peers who own homes* variable from presented models because it constrains sample size by 35% (similar to the *user cost of housing*). We display the *years parents owned* estimates, even though none are significant, because this variable does not restrict sample size.

6. In fact, *self-efficacy* is not a statistically significant mediator in any model specifications.

7. Instead of the binary homeownership indicator used in prior models, we substitute this three-category indicator of subjective current home equity.

8. We run this same analysis for physical and mental health problems, with similar results for *sense of control* mediation. For this book chapter, we present findings only for general health.

9. Another possibility is that different types of homeowners select attached versus detached dwellings. Relatedly, urban location may distinguish an attached housing effect. We suspect that in urban settings, homebuyers may be more likely to purchase townhomes and condominiums in order to take advantage of neighborhood amenities. In rural settings, the decision to purchase a townhome or condominium (rather than a single-family detached house) is more likely to be driven by the lower cost of the attached housing unit rather than by the proximity to amenities.

Conclusion

HISTORICALLY, HOMEOWNERSHIP HAS been considered an effective mechanism for wealth creation, especially for low- and moderate-income and minority households. Even with a modest down payment, homeowners can accumulate wealth through the forced savings that result from the periodic payments on fixed-rate mortgages and from rising house prices over time. The tax benefits associated with homeownership—mortgage interest and property tax deductions—can make owning less expensive than renting in many instances. Of course, the wealth-building potential of homeownership is dependent on the type of mortgage product, the timing of home purchase in the business cycle, whether households itemize tax deductions, and other factors. When lending is done right, as was the case with the CAP loans that formed the basis for the analyses in this book, low- and moderate-income households can, in fact, build wealth through a sustainable homeownership experience.

Sadly, the same cannot be said for families who used subprime mortgages to purchase homes in the run-up to the financial crisis that took place during the 2008–2010 Great Recession. In the wake of the crisis, subprime adjustable-rate loan default rates soared to 42%. At the same time, the default rate for the CAP portfolio was 6.5%.[1] The poor performance of many subprime loans had far-reaching impacts: Research has found that prime-rate borrowers who lived in neighborhoods with a high rate of subprime lending had a significantly higher risk of default than comparable borrowers living elsewhere (Ding, Quercia, & Ratcliffe 2011). Thus, subprime mortgage loans hurt entire communities, not just the low-income borrowers who were the most directly affected.

In the wake of the Great Recession, a central policy question remains: If home-ownership is not guaranteed to create wealth, are there other reasons for promoting it? Is there a rationale for supporting and extending homeownership beyond whatever financial benefits it may convey? Unfortunately, the literature on the social impacts of homeownership has not been able to provide a definitive answer to this question. One reason for this is that the social outcomes associated with homeownership can be both positive and negative. Positive aspects include those associated with greater individual benefits and broader civic and community participation. Negative aspects include the homeownership-based stratification that contributes to politics of exclusion (McCabe 2016). This exclusion leads to and is reinforced by the enactment of exclusionary zoning laws and policies that marginalize low-income households to neighborhoods with few opportunities (Dickerson 2014).

Moreover, as described in prior chapters, questions remain about which methodological strategies should be used. To what extent have past findings about homeownership been the result of methodological considerations such as selection bias? Past research on the effects of homeownership has generally failed to account for the self-selectivity of homeowners: People choose whether to buy or rent a home, and it is likely that this choice stems from a set of systematic differences between owners and renters. The failure to control for self-selection into homeownership has led to bias in analyses comparing social outcomes for homeowners and renters (Aaronson 2000; Dietz & Haurin 2003; Rohe et al. 2002).

In this book we addressed the challenge of selection bias, especially as it relates to the nonfinancial dimensions of homeownership, which are our central focus. More narrowly, we examined rigorously the positive social dimensions associated with homeownership. We conclude here by reviewing our findings and describing their implications for U.S. housing policy. In each of the chapters, we examined the relationship between homeownership and a specific social outcome while addressing the methodological challenge of selection bias. These social outcomes included physical health, financial stress, mental health, local voting participation, social capital, civic engagement, and collective efficacy. We followed these rigorous analyses with an exploration of why and how homeownership is associated with health and civic engagement.

Overall, we found that homeownership is associated with several outcomes, some of which are felt at the individual level and others at the community level. We uncovered three individual-level benefits of homeownership. First, owning a home is associated with a reduced risk of physical health problems, though financial hardship increases that risk. Homeowners experiencing financial hardship are actually at greater risk for physical health problems than their renting counterparts. Second, we found that although both low- and moderate-income renters and owners experienced similar levels of financial hardship during the Great Recession, the homeowners reported feeling more satisfied with their financial lives. Third, we found that homeownership is linked with positive mental health outcomes through the mediating factor of sense of control: The greater sense of control homeowners experience helps to explain why they report lower levels of mental health problems than renters.

Our research also uncovered four broader-reaching effects of homeownership; these also occur at the individual level, but their effects could be felt at the local neighborhood and community levels. First, we found that homeowners are more likely than renters to have voted in a recent local election, and that homeowners in disadvantaged neighborhoods are even more likely to vote than owners in other areas. Second, we found that involvement in neighborhood groups increased substantially after renters became homeowners. Our analysis of neighborhood involvement further revealed that homeowners who move are more likely to get involved in community organizations in their new neighborhoods, while renters who relocate are not. Third, we found that homeowners have more overall social capital resources and more neighborhood-based social capital resources than renters. Based on this evidence, we conclude that homeownership gives people access to social capital via increased social ties to others. Finally, we found that homeownership is associated with a higher sense of community and a greater willingness to fix neighborhood problems. These two elements form collective efficacy, which is known to reduce violent crime. Our analysis shows that through collective efficacy, homeownership is negatively associated with perceiving crime as a major neighborhood problem.

We examined possible pathways, or mechanisms, through which the benefits of homeownership are transmitted. These include one psychological mechanism (perceived control), one sociological (social identity), one financial (user cost of housing), and one having to do with residential stability. We found that sense of control was a significant factor in the health outcomes examined: An elevated sense of control explains why homeowners have a reduced risk for both physical and mental health problems, and better overall health. We also found that residential stability is a key mechanism linking homeownership and social outcomes: The longer people live in the same house, the more likely they are to vote in local elections, form social ties in their neighborhoods, and become engaged in their community. In contrast, we found that sociological and financial mechanisms play no role in explaining in the relationship between homeowners and the social outcomes we assessed. This null finding may reflect that these items were measured imperfectly. With regard to financial interests, we found that the user cost of housing is not significant in any of the models.

Additionally, we examined dependencies, or whether certain effects were altered by factors such as home equity. We found that home equity does, indeed, play a role in those models that examine health outcomes. Specifically, the homeownership effect on health depends on higher home equity; it is no longer associated with better mental, physical, and overall health when equity in the home is negative or low. This finding suggests that the relationship between homeownership and health is complicated by, and is even dependent upon, home equity levels. Future research needs to examine additional dimensions of the role of equity.

Taken as a whole, the research in this book, summarized in Table C.1, indicates that there are, indeed, nonfinancial benefits to homeownership and that while many of these consequences do occur at the household level, benefits may also extend to the broader community. These findings suggest that the social benefits of homeownership provide an important justification for continuing to support homeownership, even when its financial benefits are not guaranteed. Overall, our work adds to a body of research pointing to health and community engagement benefits associated with homeownership. Our work reveals both *which* benefits homeownership offers and *how* these are conveyed; thus we are able to raise policy recommendations, and do so in the following section.

Policy Implications

Four policy conclusions can be derived from our analyses. We describe three strategies that can be used to enhance the long-term homeownership experience, something that will make it more likely for homeowners to stay in their homes longer, and thus to experience the benefits associated with residential stability: (1) strengthening our housing finance system, (2) providing credit enhancements, and (3) continuing to provide emergency funding to particularly vulnerable homeowners. We conclude with a discussion about how these mechanisms might be expanded to renters.

First, improvements to the housing finance system must prioritize the provision of sustainable mortgage products. By "sustainable," we mean mortgage products that are originated with consideration for a borrower's ability to repay so as to

TABLE C.1

Summary of Research Findings for Homeownership

Chapter	Title	Main Effects	Pathways	Dependencies
2	Physical Health Limitations and Financial Hardship	Homeownership is associated with a reduced risk of physical health problems.		
3	Financial Stress and Satisfaction	During the financial crisis, homeowners were just as financially stressed as renters, yet more satisfied with their financial situation.		
4	Mental Health and Sense of Control	Homeownership is associated with a reduced risk of mental health problems.	Sense of control explains the homeownership effect; trust in neighbors does not.	
5	Local Voting	Homeowners are more likely than similar renters to vote in local elections.		Local voting among homeowners is more likely in disadvantaged neighborhoods.
6	Civic Engagement	After purchasing homes, renters become more involved in community affairs than do renters who also move but stay renters.		Homeownership effect is stronger for more recent homebuyers.

7	Social Capital	Homeowners have more social capital resources, both overall and within neighborhoods.	Neighborhood group involvement partially explains the homeownership effect.	
8	Collective Efficacy and Perceived Crime	Homeowners have higher levels of collective efficacy, as measured by sense of community and a willingness to fix neighborhood problems.	Collective efficacy mediates the homeownership effect, which is a negative association with perceptions of neighborhood crime.	
9	Homeownership: Mechanisms and Dependencies	Homeownership continues to be linked to health, voting, and civic engagement even when controlling for dwelling and neighborhood characteristics.	Residential stability and sense of control underlie the homeownership effect.	Effect of homeownership is stronger in attached dwellings such as condominiums and townhomes. Sense of control mediation of homeownership depends upon higher home equity.

enhance the likelihood of a successful homeownership experience. The CAP mortgages that form the basis for the analyses in this book, and similar loans originated under the auspices of the Community Reinvestment Act, are great examples of sustainable mortgage products.

All of the homeowners who participated in the CAP program received prime, fixed-rate, 30-year mortgages with a 38% debt-to-income limit. The CAP loans also had flexible features, such as low down payments, that allowed lower-income and minority families to achieve their goal of sustainable homeownership. The social benefits of homeownership will not be enjoyed if buyers cannot remain in their homes, so we support policy changes that allow homebuyers to obtain sustainable mortgage products that do not create financial strain in the short or long term.[2]

A key unfinished policy consideration is the future of the government-sponsored enterprises (GSEs) Fannie Mae and Freddie Mac. The GSEs have been in conservatorship by the federal government since 2008, and although some call for their elimination, there are many unanswered questions related to what type of institutions would replace them. Whatever is done to the GSEs themselves, there is a need to put in place mechanisms to continue the provision of liquidity, the standardization of affordable and sustainable mortgage products, and the generation of new products and risk management strategies to extend homeownership opportunities more broadly. Secondary market mechanisms that enhance the availability of sustainable mortgage credit to more households will enhance the homeownership experience by helping to ensure the quality of mortgage products.

Second, it is important to strengthen the likelihood that borrowers can sustain homeownership over time through credit enhancement mechanisms. One such mechanism is homeownership education and counseling. Policymakers should make homeownership education and counseling a requirement for all first-time homebuyers. Counseling can make home purchasers more aware about the importance of budgeting, regular savings, paying their bills on time, and undertaking regular maintenance and can increase the sustainability and stability of the homeownership experience. Although early studies suggest that only in-person counseling is effective, the online educational offerings have changed and improved over time. However, until empirically rigorous studies confirm the viability of online counseling, policymakers should require all buyers to receive in-person counseling offered by certified programs with standardized curricula. Requiring homeownership education and counseling for mortgage lending can enhance

> This is the wrong location, it's too much of a fixer-upper with outdated plumbing and electrical. We bought impulsively and didn't seek counsel. We took for granted the mortgage closing process.

the sustainability of homeownership, thus making the realization of the social benefits identified in this book more likely.

Third, policymakers can enhance the long-term sustainability of homeownership among lower-income borrowers by providing access to emergency funds. Access to emergency funds can help homeowners weather a disruption in employment, unexpected medical expenses, or other financial hardships. Communities are already making strides in this area; for example, some states have property tax relief mechanisms to help aging homeowners stay in their homes. This type of mechanism can be put into place more broadly, so that homeowners, old as well as young, experiencing crises can defer property tax payments until they get back on their feet. Another example is the Hardest Hit Fund program, established in 2010 to help homeowners who lost their jobs as a result of the financial crisis. Under the program, the government makes the mortgage payments of unemployed borrowers for up to 18 months (the program puts a lien on the property until the debt is repaid). Emergency funds can reduce psychological stress and its related health impacts during economic downturns and can enhance the residential stability at the root of some of the social benefits we examined.

Expanding the Social Impacts of Homeownerships to Renters

Finally, our findings suggest ways in which some of the social benefits associated with homeownership can be made available for renters. Two findings can be particularly useful in formulating policy: the importance of residential stability and of one's sense of control. We should subsidize residential stability rather than homeownership per se. This could be accomplished with longer rental leases for those desiring to put down roots in a community without purchasing a home. While long-term leases are common in other countries, consideration of this option would be beneficial for both U.S. renters and the communities in which they live.

Similarly, because sense of control is so important in conveying the health benefits associated with homeownership, rental leases could be structured to give renters more control over their environment. Leases could, for example, allow long-term residents to make small modifications to their unit such as painting a room or adding shelves to a storage area (the tenant would be responsible for leaving the rental unit in the same condition that existed at the time of move-in unless the property owner wants the changes to remain). Furthermore, providing incentives to tenants who maintain or improve the quality of rental properties could create value for both landlords and tenants alike: Landlords would see financial gains and renters would have better access to housing that meets their needs. One successful example of such an initiative is Cincinnati's unique experiment in renter equity. The nonprofit entity Cornerstone Corporation for Shared Equity has been offering a renter's equity program for years: "Residents fulfill commitments in their lease agreement: work assignments on the property, making timely rent payments, following house rules and participating in tenants' meetings ... In return, they earn financial credits that they can exchange for cash after five years. Renters can earn up to $10,000 over 10 years" (Clark 2015).

Looking Forward

These four policy recommendations—promoting the availability of sustainable mortgage credit through effective reform of the housing finance system (Fannie Mae and Freddie Mac), requiring housing counseling and coaching for first-time homebuyers, providing emergency funds, and expanding control and residential stability for renters—are informed by the analyses presented in this book. Grounding our recommendations on data and research, we believe that it is possible to improve the lives of Americans through strategic policy changes.

In closing, the research presented in this book shows that there is something about owning a home that is associated with positive individual, family, and community outcomes, benefits that extend beyond mere financial self-interest. However, our research also shows that the factors behind these positive benefits could be made available to renters. In the aftermath of the Great Recession, we hope that these social dimensions of homeownership will be given weight in our debates on the future of the housing finance system, the promotion of homeownership, and housing policy in general. Our communities will be stronger as a result.

Notes

1. These default rates come from the first quarter of 2010. The CAP rate comes from analysis of the CAPS data; the subprime adjustable-rate mortgage figure comes from the Mortgage Bankers Association National Delinquency Survey, which is available through Moody's Databuffet.

2. The definitions of "qualified mortgage" for lenders and "qualified residential mortgage" for secondary market entities that came about as a result of the Dodd-Frank Act were designed to encourage all players in the market to promote sustainable lending products and practices, including effective loan servicing.

Afterword

Economic opportunity and mobility in the United States have diminished for many over the past generation, undermining the nation's economic growth, dramatically unsettling our politics, and even challenging our cultural identity—as a nation of strivers in a land that gives everyone a fair shot.

Analysts have pointed out, for example, that the likelihood of a child outearning their parents has been dramatically reduced since the 1950s. Others have shown that the homeownership rate, one of the traditional ways to build wealth, especially among low-income and minority households, is at its lowest point in almost fifty years. These trends, in turn, make it less likely that we will be able to narrow the country's large racial wealth gap, which has widened significantly over the past few decades—after a generation in which we appeared to be closing the gap. People of all backgrounds, in communities all over the nation, have serious doubts that they will be able to access the "opportunity for all" that helps define the American Dream. And this doubt has shaken their faith in business, government, and other institutions.

The political landscape, particularly at the federal level but in key States as well, changed quite dramatically after the 2016 election. Under a new federal administration, housing advocates will need to build new relationships, across divides, with each other and with policymakers, for example to make the case about why homeownership matters and what a smart and fair approach requires. In this new context, where some longstanding ideological boundaries are being transcended and others hardened, it is more important than ever to rethink and test our assumptions.

In that context, this book has addressed several fundamental questions: Is homeownership still worth it? Does promoting it matter for individual families and the wider community? And if homeownership does matter, should it be considered a core part of conversations about expanding opportunity and reducing extreme inequality? The authors pose these questions with a provocative slant: Is homeownership socially beneficial and foundational to community wellbeing *even without* household-level financial gain? Notably, in a previous book, *Regaining the Dream*, they addressed the more traditional question of financial benefits, finding that they endure in spite of the massive losses and risks tied to the foreclosure crisis and the Great Recession.

In this book, which builds on trailblazing earlier work in the 2000s, we learn that homeownership is indeed beneficial in ways that go beyond financial gain. For instance, the authors find that homeownership can lead to better health outcomes, a higher likelihood of voting in local elections, a greater likelihood of taking steps toward civic goals. This work helps us to understand the specific ways in which homeownership is associated with positive outcomes and with community wellbeing.

Extending that thought: By isolating the *mechanisms* through which homeownership generates benefits, the book offers lessons about how to extend these positive impacts, such as through an enhanced sense of control and greater residential stability, more broadly to renters. Some of these policy ideas, such as longer and more flexible leases for renters, or stronger tenant protections against unlawful or arbitrary eviction, can help advocates and entrepreneurs in both the public and private sectors strategize and make changes in their communities.

At the Ford Foundation, we support research projects such as this one because we believe that influential assumptions need to be bolstered—and sometimes corrected—by facts and thoughtful scholarship. As underscored by leading international organizations and Nobel-prize-winning economists, the empirical evidence is that inequality, particularly when it reaches extreme levels, affects us all, not just the disadvantaged—that it undermines economic growth and broader measures of wellbeing. The important body of work reported in this book corroborates that finding. Homeownership can indeed help families succeed and thrive. The next question becomes how to share such benefits more broadly.

We will need to work together within the field of housing, to be sure, but we will also need to reach people in health, education, finance, workforce development, and other fields. A new generation of partnerships can be based on the notion of housing as the hub in the opportunity wheel or, as some would have it, of "housing as a platform" for well-being and success (Castro 2017; Kelly & Karnas 2014). As this book so powerfully reveals, what's good for the family pocketbook is often very good in other ways as well—and is worth expanding across the community.

Xavier de Souza Briggs,
Vice President, Economic Opportunity and Markets,
The Ford Foundation

References

Aaronson, Daniel. 2000. A note on the benefits of homeownership. *Journal of Urban Economics* 47(3):356–369.

Abbott, Stephen. 2007. The psychosocial effects on health of socioeconomic inequalities. *Critical Public Health* 17(2):151–158.

Alford, Robert R., & Harry M. Scoble. 1968. Sources of local political involvement. *American Political Science Review* 62(4):1192–1206.

Alley, Dawn E., Jennifer Lloyd, Jose A. Pagan, Craig E. Pollack, Michelle Shardell, & Carolyn Cannuscio. 2011. Mortgage delinquency and changes in access to health resources and depressive symptoms in a nationally representative cohort of Americans older than 50 years. *American Journal of Public Health* 101(12):2293–2298.

Anily, Shoshana, Jacob Hornik, & Miron Israeli. 1999. Inferring the distribution of households' duration of residence from data on current residence time. *Journal of Business & Economic Statistics* 17(3):373–381.

Antonakis, John, Samuel Bendahan, Philippe Jacquart, & Rafael Lalive. 2010. On making causal claims: A review and recommendations. *Leadership Quarterly* 21(6):1086–1120.

Balfour, Danny L., & Janet L. Smith. 1996. Transforming lease-purchase housing programs for low income families: Towards empowerment and engagement. *Journal of Urban Affairs* 18(2):173–188.

Bandura, A. 2000. Exercise of human agency through collective efficacy. *Current Directions in Psychological Science* 9(3):75–78.

Barker, David R. 2013. The evidence does not show that homeownership benefits children. *Cityscape* 15(2):231–234.

Bartley, Mel. 1994. Unemployment and ill health: Understanding the relationship. *Journal of Epidemiology and Community Health* 48(4):333–337.

Bellair, P. E., & C. R. Browning. 2010. Contemporary disorganization research: An assessment and further test of the systemic model of neighborhood crime. *Journal of Research in Crime and Delinquency* 47(4):496–521.

Belsky, Eric S., & Mark Duda. 2002. Asset appreciation, timing of purchases and sales, and returns to low-income homeownership. In Nicolas P. Retsinas & Eric S. Belsky, eds., *Low-income homeownership: Examining the unexamined goal* (pp. 208–238). Washington, DC: Brookings Institution Press.

Bennett, Gary G., Melissa Scharoun-Lee, & Reginald Tucker-Seeley. 2009. Will the public's health fall victim to the home foreclosure epidemic? *PLoS Medicine* 6(6):e1000087.

Benson, Michael L., Greer L. Fox, Alfred DeMaris, & Judy Van Wyk. 2003. Neighborhood disadvantage, individual economic distress and violence against women in intimate relationships. *Journal of Quantitative Criminology* 19(3):207–235.

Berry, B. and J. Kasarda. 1977. *Contemporary Urban Ecology*. New York: Macmillan.

Boehm, T. P. 1981. Tenure choice and expected mobility: A synthesis. *Journal of Urban Economics* 10:375–389.

Bostic, R. W., & K. O. Lee. 2009. Homeownership: America's cream? In R. M. Blank & M. S. Barr, eds., *Insufficient funds: Savings, assets, credit, and banking among low-income households*. New York: Russell Sage Foundation.

Bourdieu, Pierre. 1977. *Outline of a theory of practice* (Vol. 16). Cambridge: Cambridge University Press.

Brady, Henry E., Sidney Verba, & Kay Lehman Schlozman. 1995. Beyond SES: A resource model of political participation. *American Political Science Review* 89(2):271–294.

Brown, Barbara, Douglas D. Perkins, & Graham Brown. 2003. Place attachment in a revitalizing neighborhood: Individual and block levels of analysis. *Journal of Environmental Psychology* 23(3):259–271.

Bucks, B. K., A. B. Kennickell, T. L. Mach, & K. B. Moore. 2009. Changes in U.S. family finances from 2004–2007: Evidence from the Survey of Consumer Finances. *Federal Reserve Bulletin* 95.

Burr, Jeffrey A., Francis G. Caro, & Jennifer Moorhead. 2002. Productive aging and civic participation. *Journal of Aging Studies* 16(1):87–105.

Bursik, Robert J. 1988. Social disorganization and theories of crime and delinquency: Problems and prospects. *Criminology* 26(4):519–552.

Carson, Arlene J., Neena L. Chappell, & Carren E. Dujela. 2010. Power dynamics and perceptions of neighbourhood attachment and involvement: Effects of length of residency versus home ownership. *Housing, Theory and Society* 27(2):162–177.

Castro, Julian. 2017. Housing as a Platform for Opportunity: Memo to the American People. Washington D.C.: U.S. Department of Housing and Urban Development. Accessed January 11, 2017: https://portal.hud.gov/hudportal/documents/huddoc?id=HUDExitMemo010517.pdf.

Chavis, David M., James H. Hogge, David W. McMillan, & Abraham Wandersman. 1986. Sense of community through Brunswik's lens: A first look. *Journal of Community Psychology* 14(1):24–40.

Clark, Anna. 2015. "Renters are Getting a Stake in Cleveland Real Estate." *NextCity.org*. https://nextcity.org/daily/entry/Cleveland (accessed February 12, 2017).

Coffé, Hilde. 2009. Social capital and community heterogeneity. *Social Indicators Research* 91(2):155–170.

Coffé, Hilde, & Benny Geys. 2006. Community heterogeneity: A burden for the creation of social capital? *Social Science Quarterly* 87(5):1053–1072.

Cohen, S., T. Kamarck, & R. Mermelstein. 1983. A global measure of perceived stress. *Journal of Health and Social Behavior* 24(4):385–396.

Collins, J. Michael, & Collin M. O'Rourke. 2010. Financial education and counseling—Still holding promise. *Journal of Consumer Affairs* 44(3):483–498.

Cook, Thomas D., & Donald Thomas Campbell. 1979. *Quasi-experimentation: Design & analysis issues for field settings*. Boston: Houghton Mifflin.

Cox, K. R. 1982. Housing tenure and neighborhood activism. *Urban Affairs Review* 18(1):107.

Darley, John M., & Bibb Latane. 1968. Bystander intervention in emergencies: Diffusion of responsibility. *Journal of Personality and Social Psychology* 8(4p1):377.

Davis, John Emmeus. 1991. *Contested ground: Collective action and the urban neighborhood*. Ithaca, NY: Cornell University Press.

Dickerson, Mechele. 2014. *Homeownership and America's financial underclass: Flawed premises, broken promises, new prescriptions*. Cambridge: Cambridge University Press.

Diehr, Paula, Lu Chen, Donald Patrick, Ziding Feng, & Yutaka Yasui. 2005. Reliability, effect size, and responsiveness of health status measures in the design of randomized and cluster-randomized trials. *Contemporary Clinical Trials* 26(1):45–58.

Dietz, R. D. 2002. The estimation of neighborhood effects in the social sciences: An interdisciplinary approach. *Social Science Research* 3(4):539–575.

Dietz, R. 2003. The Social Consequences of Homeownership. *Journal of Urban Economics* 54:401–450.

Dietz, R. D., & D. R. Haurin. 2003. The social and private micro-level consequences of homeownership. *Journal of Urban Economics* 54(3):401–450.

Ding, Lei, Roberto G. Quercia, Wei Li, & Janneke Ratcliffe. 2011. Risky borrowers or risky mortgages: Disaggregating effects using propensity score models. *Journal of Real Estate Research* 33(2):245–277.

DiPasquale, Denise, & Edward L. Glaeser. 1999. Incentives and Social Capital: Are Homeowners Better Citizens? *Journal of Urban Economics* 45(2):354–84.

Doling, John F., & Bruce Stafford. 1989. *Home ownership: The diversity of experience* (Vol. 5). Farnham, UK: Gower Publishing Company.

Drentea, Patricia, & Paul J. Lavrakas. 2000. Over the limit: The association among health, race and debt. *Social Science & Medicine* 50(4):517–529.

Dunn, James R. 2000. Housing and health inequalities: Review and prospects for research. *Housing Studies* 15(3):341–366.

Dupuis, Ann, & David C. Thorns. 1998. Home, home ownership and the search for ontological security. *Sociological Review* 46(1):24–47.

Dwyer, Rachel E., Lisa A. Neilson, Michael Nau, & Randy Hodson. 2016. Mortgage worries: Young adults and the US housing crisis. *Socio-Economic Review* 14(3):483–505.

Elo, Anna-Liisa, Anneli Leppänen, & Antti Jahkola. 2003. Validity of a single-item measure of stress symptoms. *Scandinavian Journal of Work, Environment & Health* 29(6):444–451.

Engelhardt, G. V., M. D. Eriksen, W. G. Gale, & G. B. Mills. 2010. What are the social benefits of homeownership? Experimental evidence for low-income households. *Journal of Urban Economics* 67(3):249–258.

Epp, Charles R, Steven Maynard-Moody, & Donald P Haider-Markel. 2014. *Pulled over: How police stops define race and citizenship*. Chicago: University of Chicago Press.

Federal Reserve Flow of Funds Report, Table B.100 Balance Sheets of Households and NonProfit Organizations. March 11, 2010.

Fischel, William A. 2001. *The homevoter hypothesis: How home values influence local government taxation, school finance, and land-use policies.* Cambridge, MA: Harvard University Press.

Forrest, Ray, & Alan Murie. 1991. Transformation through tenure? The early purchasers of council houses 1968–1973. *Journal of Social Policy* 20(1):1–25.

Frank, Kenneth A., Yong Zhao, & Kathryn Borman. 2004. Social capital and the diffusion of innovations within organizations: The case of computer technology in schools. *Sociology of Education* 77(2):148–171.

Froot, Kenneth A. 1989. Consistent covariance matrix estimation with cross-sectional dependence and heteroskedasticity in financial data. *Journal of Financial and Quantitative Analysis* 24(3):333–355.

Fry, R. & R. Kochar. America's wealth gap between middle-income and upper-income families is widest on record. Pew Research: 17 December 2014. Accessed 13 February 2017: http://www.pewresearch.org/fact-tank/2014/12/17/wealth-gap-upper-middle-income/.

Fuller-Thomson, Esme, J. David Hulchanski, & Stephen Hwang. 2000. The housing/health relationship: What do we know? *Reviews on Environmental Health* 15(1-2):109–134.

Furstenberg Jr., Frank F., & Mary Elizabeth Hughes. 1995. Social capital and successful development among at-risk youth. *Journal of Marriage and the Family* 57(3):580–592.

Furstenburg, F. F. 1993. How families manage risk and opportunity in dangerous neighborhoods. In W. J. Wilson, ed., *Sociology and the public agenda* (pp. 231–258). Newbury Park, CA: Sage.

Galster, George C. 1987. *Homeowners and neighborhood reinvestment.* Durham, NC: Duke University Press.

Geis, Karlyn and Catherine Ross. 1998. A New Look at Urban Alienation: The Effect of Neighborhood Disorder on Perceived Powerlessness. *Social Psychology Quarterly* 61:232–246.

Gilderbloom, John I., & John P. Markham. 1995. The impact of homeownership on political beliefs. *Social Forces* 73(4):1589–1607.

Gladow, Nancy Wells, & Margaret P. Ray. 1986. The impact of informal support systems on the wellbeing of low-income single parents. *Family Relations* 35(1):113–123.

Glaeser, E. L. 2001. The formation of social capital. In J. F. Helliwell (Ed.), *The contribution of human and social capital to sustained economic growth and well-being: International symposium report* (pp. 381–393). Quebec: Human Resources Development Center.

Glaeser, Edward, David Laibson, and Bruce Sacerdote. 2000. "The Economic Approach to Social Capital", *NBER working paper, No. 7728.* Cambridge: National Bureau of Economic Research.

Glaeser, E. L., D. Laibson, & B. Sacerdote. 2002. An economic approach to social capital. *The Economic Journal* 112:F437–F458.

Glaeser, Edward L., & Bruce Sacerdote. 2000. *The social consequences of housing.* Cambridge, MA: National Bureau of Economic Research.

Granovetter, Mark S. 1973. The strength of weak ties. *American Journal of Sociology* 78(6):1360–1380.

Green, Richard, Gary Painter, & Michelle White. 2012. *Measuring the benefits of homeowning: Effects on children redux.* Research Institute for Housing America Research Paper (12-01).

Green, Richard K., & Susan M. Wachter. 2005. The American mortgage in historical and international context. *Journal of Economic Perspectives* 19(4):93–114.

Guest, Avery M., & R. Salvador Oropesa. 1986. Informal social ties and political activity in the metropolis. *Urban Affairs Review* 21(4):550–574.

Guo, Shenyang, & Mark Fraser. 2009. *Propensity score analysis*. Thousand Oaks, CA: Sage Publications.

Hartig, Terry, & Roderick J. Lawrence. 2003. Introduction: The residential context of health. *Journal of Social Issues* 59(3):455–473.

Haurin, D. R., Dietz, Robert D., & Weinberg, Bruce A. 2005. The Impact of Neighborhood Homeownership Rates: A Review of The Theoretical and Empirical Literature (September 1, 2003). *Economics of Innovation and New Technology* 14(5).

Haurin, Donald R., Toby L. Parcel, & R. Jean Haurin. 2002. Does homeownership affect child outcomes? *Real Estate Economics* 30(4):635–666.

Hayden, Dolores. 2003. *Building suburbia: Green fields and urban growth, 1820–2000* (1st ed.). New York: Pantheon Books.

Henderson, J. V., & Y. M. Ioannides. 1989. Dynamic aspects of consumer decisions in housing markets. *Journal of Urban Economics* 26:212–230.

Herbert, C. E., & E. S. Belsky. 2008. The homeownership experience of low-income and minority households: A review and synthesis of the literature. *Cityscape* 10(2):5–60.

Herbert, C. E., D. R. Haurin, S. S. Rosenthal, & M. Duda. 2005. Homeownership Gaps Among Low-Income and Minority Borrowers and Neighborhoods. Christopher E Herbert, Donald R. Haurin, Stuart S. Rosenthal, and Mark Duda. Prepared for the U.S. Department of Housing and Urban Development.

Hirschman, A. O. 1970. *Exit, voice, and loyalty; responses to decline in firms, organizations, and states*. Cambridge, MA: Harvard University Press.

Hiscock, Rosemary, Ade Kearns, Sally MacIntyre, & Anne Ellaway. 2001. Ontological security and psycho-social benefits from the home: Qualitative evidence on issues of tenure. *Housing, Theory and Society* 18(1-2):50–66.

Hiscock, R., S. Macintyre, A. Kearns, & A. Ellaway. 2003. Residents and Residence: Factors Predicting the Health Disadvantage of Social Renters Compared to Owner-Occupiers. *Journal of Social Issues* 59:527–546.

Holbrook, Thomas M., & Aaron C. Weinschenk. 2014. Campaigns, Mobilization, and Turnout in Mayoral Elections. *Political Research Quarterly* 67(1):42–55.

Jenkinson, Crispin, Richard Layte, Damian Jenkinson, Kate Lawrence, Sophie Petersen, Colin Paice, & John Stradling. 1997. A shorter form health survey: Can the SF-12 replicate results from the SF-36 in longitudinal studies? *Journal of Public Health* 19(2):179–186.

Kasarda, John D., & Morris Janowitz. 1974. Community attachment in mass society. *American Sociological Review* 39(3):328–339.

Kellett, J. 1989. Health and Housing. *Journal of Psychosomatic Research* 33:255–268.

Kelly, B. & F. Karnas. 2014. Affordable Housing as a Platform for Resident Success: Building the Evidence Base. In *What Counts: Harnessing Data for America's Communities*, eds. Naomi Cytron, David J. Erickson, and G. Thomas Kingsley. Accessed January 11, 2017: http://www.whatcountsforamerica.org/portfolio/affordable-housing-as-a-platform-for-resident-success-building-the-evidence-base/.

Kim, Yong-Chan, & Sandra J. Ball-Rokeach. 2006. Community storytelling network, neighborhood context, and civic engagement: A multilevel approach. *Human Communication Research* 32(4):411–439.

Kingston, Paul William, John L. P. Thompson, & Douglas M. Eichar. 1984. The politics of homeownership. *American Politics Quarterly* 12(2):131–150.

Kochhar, Rakesh, Richard Fry, & Paul Taylor. 2011. *Twenty to one: Wealth gaps rise to record highs between whites, blacks and Hispanics*. Washington, DC: Pew Research Center. http://www.pewsocialtrends.org/.../wealth-gaps-rise-to-record-highs-between-whites-blacks-hispanics (accessed November 28, 2016).

Kornhauser, Ruth Rosner. 1978. *Social sources of delinquency: An appraisal of analytic models*. Chicago: University of Chicago Press.

Kuo, Frances E., William C. Sullivan, Rebekah Levine Coley, & Liesette Brunson. 1998. Fertile ground for community: Inner-city neighborhood common spaces. *American Journal of Community Psychology* 26(6):823–851.

Ladd, E.C. 1996. The Data Just Don't Show Erosion of America's "Social Capital," *The Public Perspective* 5–22.

Latkin, Carl A., & Aaron D. Curry. 2003. Stressful neighborhoods and depression: A prospective study of the impact of neighborhood disorder. *Journal of Health and Social Behavior* 44(1):34–44.

Lawless, Jennifer L., & Richard L. Fox. 2001. Political participation of the urban poor. *Social Problems* 48(3):362–385.

Lee, Matthew R., & John P. Bartkowski. 2004. Love thy neighbor? Moral communities, civic engagement, and juvenile homicide in rural areas. *Social Forces* 82(3):1001–1035.

Lee, B. A., Oropesa, R. S., & Kanan, J. W. 1994. Neighborhood context and residential mobility. *Demography* 31: 249–270.

Lin, Nan. 1999. Social networks and status attainment. *Annual Review of Sociology* 25:467–487.

Lin, Nan, Karen S. Cook, & Ronald S. Burt. 2001. *Social capital: Theory and research* New Brunswick, NJ: Transaction Publishers.

* Lindblad, M., K. Manturuk, & R. Quercia. Sense of Community and Informal Social Control among Lower Income Households: The Role of Homeownership and Collective Efficacy in Reducing Subjective Neighborhood Crime and Disorder. *American Journal of Community Psychology* 51(1):123–139.

* Lindblad, Mark R., & Roberto G. Quercia. 2015. Why is homeownership associated with nonfinancial benefits? A path analysis of competing mechanisms. *Housing Policy Debate* 25(2):263–288.

Lindblad, Mark R., & Sarah F. Riley. 2015. Loan modifications and foreclosure sales during the financial crisis: Consequences for health and stress. *Housing Studies* 30(7):1092–1115.

Lindblad, M. R., Han, H., Yu, S., and Rohe, W. M. (2017). First-Time Homebuying: Attitudes and Behaviors of Low-Income Renters through the Financial Crisis. *Housing Studies*, in press.

Locke, John. 1689. *Two treatises of government* (3rd ed.). London: Black Swan.

Long, D. A., & D. D. Perkins. 2007. Community social and place predictors of sense of community: A multilevel and longitudinal analysis. *Journal of Community Psychology* 35(5):563–581.

Macleod, John, & G. Davey Smith. 2003. Psychosocial factors and public health: A suitable case for treatment? *Journal of Epidemiology and Community Health* 57(8):565–570.

Makin, John H. 2013. The global financial crisis and American wealth accumulation: The Fed needs a bubble watch. *Economic Outlook*. Available at http://www.aei.org/wp-content/uploads/2013/08/-the-global-financial-crisis-and-american-wealth-accumulation-the-fed-needs-a-bubble-watch_142746530114.pdf.

* Manturuk, K., S. Riley, & J. Ratcliffe 2012. Perception vs. reality: The relationship between low-income homeownership, perceived financial stress, and financial hardship. *Social science research* 41(2):276–286.

* Manturuk, Kim R. 2012. Urban Homeownership and Mental Health: Mediating Effect of Perceived Sense of Control. *City & Community* 11(4):409–430.

* Manturuk, K., M. Lindblad & R. Quercia. 2009. Homeownership and local voting in disadvantaged urban neighborhoods. *Cityscape* 11(3):213–230.

* Manturuk, K., M. Lindblad, & R. Quercia. Homeownership and Civic Engagement in Low-Income Urban Neighborhoods: A Longitudinal Analysis. *Urban Affairs Review* 48(5):731–760.

* Manturuk, K., M. Lindblad, & R. Quercia. 2010. Friends and Neighbors: Homeownership and Social Capital Among Low- to Moderate-Income Families. *Journal of Urban Affairs* 32(4):471–488.

Massey, Douglas S. 1990. American Apartheid: Segregation and the Making of the Underclass. *The American Journal of Sociology* 96:329–357.

McBride, Amanda Moore, Margaret S. Sherraden, & Suzanne Pritzker. 2006. Civic engagement among low-income and low-wealth families: In their words. *Family Relations* 55(2):152–162.

McCabe, Brian J. 2016. *No place like home: Wealth, community, and the politics of homeownership.* New York: Oxford University Press.

McLaughlin, Katie A., Arijit Nandi, K. M. Keyes, Monica Uddin, Allison E. Aiello, Sandro Galea, K. C. Koenen, L. Y. Abramson, G. I. Metalsky, & L. B. Alloy. 2012. Home foreclosure and risk of psychiatric morbidity during the recent financial crisis. *Psychological Medicine* 42(7):1441.

McMillan, D. W., & D. M Chavis. 1986. Sense of community: A definition and theory. *Journal of Community Psychology* 14(1):6–23.

Megbolugbe, Isaac F., & Peter D. Linneman. 1993. Home ownership. *Urban Studies* 30(4-5):659–682.

Messner, Steven F., Eric P. Baumer, & Richard Rosenfeld. 2004. Dimensions of social capital and rates of criminal homicide. *American Sociological Review* 69(6):882–903.

Mingche, M. Li. 1977. A Logit Model of Homeownership. *Econometrica* 45:1081–1097.

Moeller, Sabine, & Kristina Wittkowski. 2010. The burdens of ownership: Reasons for preferring renting. *Managing Service Quality: An International Journal* 20(2):176–191.

Nettleton, Sarah, & Roger Burrows. 1998. Mortgage debt, insecure home ownership and health: An exploratory analysis. *Sociology of Health & Illness* 20(5):731–753.

Newman, Sandra J., & C. Scott Holupka. 2013. Looking back to move forward in homeownership research. *Cityscape* 15(2):235–246.

Northridge, Mary E., Elliot D. Sclar, & Padmini Biswas. 2003. Sorting out the connections between the built environment and health: A conceptual framework for navigating pathways and planning healthy cities. *Journal of Urban Health* 80(4):556–568.

Office of Policy Development and Research. 2016. Neighborhoods and Violent Crime. In *Evidence Matters.* Washington D.C.: U.S. Department of Housing and Urban Development. Available: https://www.huduser.gov/portal/periodicals/em/summer16/highlight2.html.

Oh, Joong-Hwan. 2004. Race/ethnicity, homeownership, and neighborhood attachment. *Race and Society* 7(2):63–77.

Oliver, J. Eric. 1999. The effects of metropolitan economic segregation on local civic participation. *American Journal of Political Science* 43(1):186–212.

Orbell, John M., & Toru Uno. 1972. A theory of neighborhood problem solving: Political action vs. residential mobility. *American Political Science Review* 66(2):471–489.

Pappas, Gregory, Susan Queen, Wilbur Hadden, & Gail Fisher. 1993. The increasing disparity in mortality between socioeconomic groups in the United States, 1960 and 1986. *New England Journal of Medicine* 329(2):103–109.

Perin, Constance. 1977. *Everything in Its Place: Social Order and Land Use in America.* Princeton, NJ: Princeton University Press.

Perrin, Andrew J. 2006. *Citizen speak.* Chicago: University of Chicago Press.

Portes, Alejandro. 2000. Social capital: Its origins and applications in modern sociology. In Eric L. Lesser, ed., *Knowledge and social capital* (pp. 43–67). Boston: Butterworth-Heinemann.

Pratt, G. 1986. Housing tenure and social cleavages in urban Canada. *Annals of the Association of American Geographers* 76:366–380.

Pratt, G. 1987. Class, home, and politics. *Canadian Review of Sociology and Anthropology* 24(1):39–57.

Putnam, Robert D. 1995. Tuning in, tuning out: The strange disappearance of social capital in America. *PS: Political Science & Politics* 28(4):664–683.

Putnam, Robert D. 2000. *Bowling Alone: The Collapse and Revival of American Community.* New York: Simon and Schuster.

Quercia, Roberto, Allison Freeman, and Janneke Ratcliffe. 2011. *Regaining the Dream: How to Renew the Promise of Homeownership for America's Families.* Washington D.C.: Brookings Institution Press.

Quercia, R. G., & J. Ratcliffe. 2010. The preventable foreclosure crisis. *Housing Policy Debate* 20(4):743–749.

Quercia, Roberto, & Jonathan Spader. 2008. Does homeownership counseling affect the prepayment and default behavior of affordable mortgage borrowers? *Journal of Policy Analysis and Management* 27(2):304–325.

Riley, Sarah F., HongYu Ru, & Qing Feng. 2013. The user cost of low-income homeownership. *Journal of Regional Analysis and Policy* 43(2):123–137.

Riley, Sarah F., Hongyu Ru, & Roberto G. Quercia. 2009. The community advantage program database: Overview and comparison with the current population survey. *Cityscape* 11(3):247–256.

Roach, Jack L., & Orville R. Gursslin. 1965. The lower class, status frustration and social disorganization. *Social Forces* 43(4):501–510.

Rohe, W. M., & M. R. Lindblad. 2014. Reexamining the social benefits of homeownership after the foreclosure crisis. In E. S. Belsky, C. E. Herbert, & J. H. Molinsky, eds., *Homeownership built to last: Balancing access, affordability, and risk after the housing crisis.* Boston: Brookings Institution Press and the Harvard University Joint Center for Housing Studies.

Rohe, W. M., & S. Mouw. 1991. The Politics of Relocation: The Moving of the Crest Street Community. *Journal of the American Planning Association* 57(1):57–68.

Rohe, W. M., & M. A. Stegman. 1994a. The effects of homeownership on the self-esteem, perceived control and life satisfaction of low-income people. *Journal of the American Planning Association* 60(2):173–184.

Rohe, W. M., & M. A. Stegman. 1994b. The impact of home ownership on the social and political involvement of low-income people. *Urban Affairs Review* 30(1):152.

Rohe, W. M., & L. S. Stewart. 1996. Homeownership and neighborhood stability. *Housing Policy Debate* 7(1):37–81.

Rohe, William M., & Victoria Basolo. 1997. Long-term effects of homeownership on the self-perceptions and social interaction of low-income persons. *Environment and Behavior* 29(6):793–819.

Rohe, William, Shannon Van Zandt, and George McCarthy. 2000. The Social Benefits and Costs of Homeownership: A Critical Assessment of the Research. Working paper 00-01. Washington, DC: Research Institute for Housing America: 1–30.

Rohe, William M., Shannon Van Zandt, & George McCarthy. 2002. Homeownership and access to opportunity. *Housing Studies* 17(1):51–61.

Roncek, Dennis W., Ralph Bell, & Jeffrey M. A. Francik. 1981. Housing projects and crime: Testing a proximity hypothesis. *Social Problems* 29(2):151–166.

Rosenbaum, Emily. 1996. Racial/ethnic differences in home ownership and housing quality, 1991. *Social Problems* 43(4):403–426.

Ross, C. E. 2000. Neighborhood disadvantage and adult depression. *Journal of Health and Social Behavior* 41(2):177–187.

Ross, C. E., & J. Mirowsky. 2001. Neighborhood disadvantage, disorder, and health. *Journal of Health and Social Behavior* 42(3):258–276.

Ross, C. E., J. Mirowsky, & S. Pribesh. 2001. Powerlessness and the amplification of threat: Neighborhood disadvantage, disorder, and mistrust. *American Sociological Review* 66(4):568–591.

Rossi, Peter H., & Eleanor Weber. 1996. The social benefits of homeownership: Empirical evidence from national surveys. *Housing Policy Debate* 7(1):1–35.

Rothwell, Jonathan T. 2010. Trust in diverse, integrated, cities: A revisionist perspective. *SSRN Electronic Journal.*

Rotolo, T., J. Wilson, & M. E. Hughes. 2010. Homeownership and volunteering: An alternative approach to studying social inequality and civic engagement. *Sociological Forum* 25(3):570–587.

Sampson, R. J. 1988. Local Friendship Ties and Community Attachment in Mass Society: A Multilevel Systemic Model. *American Sociological Review* 3:766–779.

Sampson, R. J. 1991. Linking the Micro- and Macro-level Dimensions of Community Social Organization. *Social Forces* 70:43–64.

Sampson, R. J. 2009. Racial Stratification and the Durable Tangle of Neighborhood Inequality. *ANNALS of the American Academy of Political and Social Science* 621(1):260–280.

Sampson, R. J., S. W. Raudenbush, & F. Earls. 1997. Neighborhoods and violent crime: a multilevel study of collective efficacy. *Science* 277(5328):918–924.

Sampson, Robert J., & W. Byron Groves. 1989. Community structure and crime: Testing social-disorganization theory. *American Journal of Sociology* 94(4):774–802.

Sampson, Robert J., Jeffrey D. Morenoff, & Thomas Gannon-Rowley. 2002. Assessing "neighborhood effects": Social processes and new directions in research. *Annual Review of Sociology* 28:443–478.

Sampson, Robert J., & Stephen W. Raudenbush. 1999. Systematic social observation of public spaces: A new look at disorder in urban neighborhoods. *American Journal of Sociology* 105(3):603–651.

Sampson, R. J., & Raudenbush, S. W. 2004. Seeing disorder: Neighborhood stigma and the social construction of "Broken windows". *Social Psychology Quarterly* 67(4):319–342.

Santiago, A. M., Galster, G. C., Santiago-San Roman, A. H., Tucker, C. M., Kaiser, A. A., Grace, R. A., & Linn, A. T. H. 2010. Foreclosing on the American Dream: The financial consequences of low-income homeownership. *Housing Policy Debate* 20:707–742.

Sarason, Seymour Bernard. 1974. *The psychological sense of community; prospects for a community psychology* (1st ed.). San Francisco: Jossey-Bass.

Saunders, Peter. 1978. Domestic property and social class. *International Journal of Urban and Regional Research* 2(1-4):233–251.

Schofer, E., & M. Fourcade-Gourinchas. 2001. The Structural Contexts of Civic Engagement: Voluntary Association Membership in Comparative Perspective. *American Sociological Review* 66:806–828.

Seibert, Scott E., Maria L. Kraimer, & Robert C. Liden. 2001. A social capital theory of career success. *Academy of Management Journal* 44(2):219–237.

Shaw, Clifford R., & Henry D. McKay. 1942. *Juvenile delinquency and urban areas.* Chicago: University of Chicago Press.

Skocpol, Theda. 1996. Unravelling from Above. *The American Prospect* 25:20–25.

Skocpol, Theda. 1997. The Tocqueville problem: Civic engagement in American democracy. *Social Science History* 21(4):455–479.

Skogan, Wesley. 1990. *Disorder and decline: Crime and the spiral of decay in American cities.* Berkeley: University of California Press.

Smith, David Horton. 1994. Determinants of Voluntary Association Participation and Volunteering: A Literature Review. *Nonprofit and Voluntary Sector Quarterly* 23:243–263.

Son, Joonmo, & Nan Lin. 2008. Social capital and civic action: A network-based approach. *Social Science Research* 37(1):330–349.

South, Scott J., & Glenn D. Deane. 1993. Race and residential mobility: Individual determinants and structural constraints. *Social Forces* 72(1):147–167.

Spader, Jonathan, Daniel McCue, and Christopher Herbert. 2016. *Homeowner Households and the U.S. Homeownership Rate: Tenure Projections for 2015-2035.* Cambridge, MA: Harvard Joint Center for Housing Studies.

Stack, C. 1983. *All our kin: Strategies for survival in a black community.* New York: Basic Books.

Stegman, Michael A., Roberto G. Quercia, Janneke H. Ratcliffe, Lei Ding, & Walter R. Davis. 2007. Preventive servicing is good for business and affordable homeownership policy. *Housing Policy Debate* 18(2):243–278.

Swaroop, Sapna, & Jeffrey D. Morenoff. 2006. Building community: The neighborhood context of social organization. *Social Forces* 84(3):1665–1695.

Tabachnick, Barbara and Linda Fidell. 2007. *Using Multivariate Statistics, 5th ed.* Boston: Allyn and Bacon.

Tanur, Judith M. 1992. *Questions about questions: Inquiries into the cognitive bases of surveys.* Thousand Oaks, CA: Russell Sage Foundation.

Taylor, Ralph B. 1996. Neighborhood Responses to Disorder and Local Attachments: The Systemic Model of Attachment, Social Disorganization, and Neighborhood Use Value. *Sociological Forum* 11:41–74.

Thaden, Emily, Andrew Greer, & Susan Saegert. 2013. Shared equity homeownership: A welcomed tenure alternative among lower-income households. *Housing Studies* 28(8):1175–1196.

Tocqueville, Alexis, & Henri C. M. Clérel. 1862. *Democracy in America*, tr. by H. Reeve.

Townsend, Nicholas. 2002. *Package deal: Marriage, work and fatherhood in men's lives.* Philadelphia: Temple University Press.

Turner, Tracy M., & Heather Luea. 2009. Homeownership, wealth accumulation and income status. *Journal of Housing Economics* 18(2):104–114.

Uslaner, Eric M., & Mitchell Brown. 2005. Inequality, trust, and civic engagement. *American Politics Research* 33(6):868–894.

Van De Bunt, G. (1999). Friends by choice: An actor-oriented statistical network model for friendship networks through time. Thela Thesis (Ph.D. thesis), University of Groningen, The Netherlands.

Van Der Gaag, Martin, & Tom A. B. Snijders. 2005. The resource generator: Social capital quantification with concrete items. *Social Networks* 27(1):1–29.

Verba, Sidney, Kay Schlozman, and Henry Brady. 1995. *Voice and Equality: Civic Volunteerism in American Politics*. Cambridge, MA: Harvard University Press.

Waldrip, K. 2009. Housing Affordability Trends for Working Households. Center for Housing Policy. http://www2.nhc.org/media/documents/Housing_Affordability_Trends.pdf (accessed 2/13/2017).

Ware, J., M. Kosinski, & S.D. Keller. 1996. A 12-Item Short-Form Health Survey: construction of scales and preliminary tests of reliability and validity. *Medical Care* 34(3):220–233.

Wilson, James Q., & George L. Kelling. 2015. Broken windows. In Roger G. Dunham & Geoffrey P. Alpert, eds., *Critical issues in policing: Contemporary readings* (7th ed., pp. 455–467). Long Grove, IL: Waveland Press.

Wilson, William J. 1987. *The Truly Disadvantaged: The Inner City, the Underclass, and Public Policy*. Chicago: University of Chicago Press.

Wilson, William Julius. 1996. When work disappears. *Political Science Quarterly* 111(4):567–595.

Woldoff, Rachael A. 2002. The effects of local stressors on neighborhood attachment. *Social Forces* 81(1):87–116.

Yeo, Yeong Hun, Michal Grinstein-Weiss, and Andréa Taylor. 2010. "Neighborhood Satisfaction Between Low- and Moderate-Income Homeowners and Renters: Multilevel Analysis", *Presented at the Society for Social Work and Research 14th Annual Conference*, San Francisco, CA.

Zhang, Yan, James Rohrer, Tyrone Borders & Tommie Farrell. 2007. Patient Satisfaction, Self-Rated Health Status, and Health Confidence: An Assessment of the Utility of Single-Item Questions. *American Journal of Medical Quality* 22:42–49.

* Signifies that the publication underlies a chapter in this book.

Index

Note: Page numbers followed by f and t indicate figures and tables, respectively.